OAR STUDY GUIDE
MOCK PRACTICE
TESTS

www.How2Become.com

Orders: Please contact How2Become Ltd, Suite 3, 40 Churchill Square Business Centre, Kings Hill, Kent ME19 4YU.

You can order through Amazon.co.uk under ISBN 9781912370412, via the website www.How2Become.com, Gardners or Bertrams.

ISBN: 9781912370412

First published in 2018 by How2Become Ltd.

Typeset for How2Become Ltd by Jacob Senior.

Disclaimer

Every effort has been made to ensure that the information contained within this guide is accurate at the time of publication. How2Become Ltd is not responsible for anyone failing any part of any selection process as a result of the information contained within this guide. How2Become Ltd and their authors cannot accept any responsibility for any errors or omissions within this guide, however caused. No responsibility for loss or damage occasioned by any person acting, or refraining from action, as a result of the material in this publication can be accepted by How2Become Ltd.

The information within this guide does not represent the views of any third-party service or organisation.

As part of this product you have also received FREE access to online tests that will help you to pass your OAR and US Navy tests.

To gain access, simply go to:

www.PsychometricTestsOnline.co.uk

Get more products for passing any test at:

www.How2Become.com

CONTENTS

INTRODUCTION TO YOUR GUIDE 7

What is the OAR Test? 8

TIPS FOR PASSING THE OAR TEST 11

THE OAR TEST - READING COMPREHENSION 25

Reading Comprehension Sample Questions 34

THE OAR TEST - MATHEMATICAL REASONING 47

Mathematical Reasoning Sample Questions 70

THE OAR TEST - MECHANICAL COMPREHENSION 87

Mechanical Comprehension Test - Sample Questions 103

THE OAR TEST - MOCK TEST 1 117

OAR Mock Test 1 - Reading Comprehension Test 119

OAR Mock Test 1 - Mathematical Comprehension Test 136

OAR Mock Test 1 - Mechanical Comprehension 144

OAR MOCK TEST 1 - ANSWERS 159

Reading Comprehension 160

Mathematical Comprehension 165

Mechanical Comprehension 169

THE OAR TEST - MOCK TEST 2 173

OAR Mock Test 2 - Reading Comprehension Test 174

OAR Mock Test 2 - Mathematical Comprehension Test 194

OAR Mock Test 2 - Mechanical Comprehension Test 206

OAR MOCK TEST 2 - ANSWERS 221

Reading Comprehension 222

Mathematical Comprehension 227

Mechanical Comprehension 234

A FEW FINAL WORDS... 239

INTRODUCTION TO YOUR GUIDE

Welcome to *OAR Study Guide: Mock Practice Tests*. In this book, you'll be given all of the tools you need in order to prepare for and pass the Officer Aptitude Rating test for the United States Navy.

In this book, you'll find information on the following areas:

1. An introduction to the OAR test.

2. A look at the structure of the OAR test.

3. Tips for passing the OAR test.

4. A guide to the three main sections of the OAR test: mathematics, literacy, and mechanical reasoning.

5. 2 mock test papers for the OAR.

What is the OAR Test?

The OAR (Officer Aptitude Rating) test is used by the United States Navy to assess the general skills required, as a bare minimum to become an officer in the Navy.

The OAR consists of three different tests. These are:

1. Math Skills Test - arithmetic, algebra, geometry.

2. Reading Comprehension Test - text analysis, comprehension, tone analysis, language, inferences.

3. Mechanical Comprehension Test - mass, momentum, speed, force.

In order to pass the OAR, you'll need to be proficient in these three separate areas. For this reason, we will be devoting a chapter to each of these categories.

These three tests, and the OAR, constitute the overall ASTB-E test. This is used to measure the skills of candidates for Naval Aviator and Naval Flight Officer student positions. However, if you're intending on applying for the Officer Candidate School, you only need to take the Math, Reading Comprehension, and Mechanical Comprehension tests.

The Structure of the OAR Test

As previously mentioned, the OAR is split into three sections: Math, Reading Comprehension, and Mechanical Comprehension. Consult the following table to see the time frame for each test, as well as the total number of questions:

Subject	Time Limit (minutes)	Number of Questions
Mathematical Comprehension	40	30
Reading Comprehension	30	20
Mechanical Comprehension	15	30
Total	85	80

The OAR test is multiple-choice in nature, meaning that you must choose the correct answer from a list of answer options. While this means that your choice of answers has already been narrowed down for you, this will not make the test easy. You will still have to work out and think carefully about each of your answers within a relatively short space of time.

Scoring and Passing the OAR Test

The OAR test scores candidates between 20 and 80, with 20 being the lowest score and 80 being the highest score. Generally speaking, the minimum score required to pass the OAR test is 35. However, this is just the minimum *required* to even be considered for a position. In other words, **do not aim for the bare minimum of 35 points**, since other candidates who score higher than you will be more likely to get the position.

How Will This Book Help?

In this book, you will find everything you need in order to prepare yourself as much as possible for the OAR test. This guide will focus on providing the following:

1. Tips for passing the OAR test.

2. Guidance, explanations, and sample questions for each question type you might face in the OAR test.

3. 3 mock exams for you to complete, under timed conditions, to see

how well your studying is going.

So, let's begin by taking a look at some expert tips for passing the OAR test.

TIPS FOR PASSING THE OAR TEST

If you want to pass the OAR test, you need to be equipped with a number of different skills and pieces of knowledge. This includes:

1. Understanding the different types of question in the OAR test, as well as what's expected from you as a candidate.

2. Knowing the general skills that you'll need to pass a test, so that you can apply them in the OAR.

3. Practise in each of the three tests so that you are prepared as possible for the real OAR test.

In this chapter, we're going to be focusing on tips for passing the OAR test. Bear these in mind as you work through this book, and especially when attempting the sample questions and mock exams at the end of this book.

Come Prepared

Always make sure that you have all of the equipment necessary for completing your exam. The following are things that you can take into almost any exam:

- Black pens. You should always take a few black ballpoint pens into your exam.

- Clear pencil case. Again, this might not be necessary, but bringing a pencil case can help you be more organised. Make sure it's clear though – if the exam invigilators can't see into the pencil case easily, they may confiscate it because you could be using it to hide notes and cheat!

- Bottle of water. We'll talk more about this later on, but bringing a bottle of water can help you concentrate – you don't want to get dehydrated. Remember to make sure that the bottle is clear and has no labels.

Keep Calm

Getting a handle on your nerves can be really difficult when facing an exam, but remember that this is completely normal. If you consider that doing well in your exam is very important, then it would be bizarre for you not to be at least a bit nervous. Lots of people will be going through the same thing as you, and plenty more have been in your position and have made it out of the other end in one piece. Life goes on after your tests, even if it doesn't feel like that during the heat of an exam.

Exams are stressful, and the conditions you take them in aren't pleasant either. Being stuck in a silent room for an hour or two, with nothing but a question paper and your own thoughts, can be incredibly daunting. However, you need to remember that you're not the only one who feels this way, and that a bit of nerves can give you the boost you need in the exam room.

That said, you need to keep any anxiety under control. A breakdown just before the OAR test (or even worse, during it) is uncommon, but just remember that not doing as well as you'd hoped in a single exam isn't the end of the world.

You might feel as though you aren't prepared enough. This happens often, and can be incredibly demoralising. Remember that how prepared you think you are doesn't necessarily represent how well prepared you actually are. Sometimes, people who feel poorly prepared for some exams in the minutes before taking it end up doing incredibly well, and some people find themselves doing worse in exams that they felt completely ready for. Essentially, you never truly know how prepared you are.

Besides, what's the use in worrying on the day of the test? There's no time left to go back and revise some more, so there's no point in getting stressed about it once you're in the room. Try and get into the current moment and power through it.

Here are some other tips for keeping calm in the exam:

- Breathing exercises. If you find yourself getting nervous before exams, or struggle to get to sleep due to exam anxiety, then breathing exercises could be beneficial.

- Get into the moment. Just before and during the OAR it can help to go into "exam-mode". By this, we mean blocking off outside distractions and any negativity coming from anywhere. Sometimes, having fellow candidates talk about the possible contents of the exam just before entering can put you off. It might make you feel as if you've missed out on something major, and then cause you to worry once you enter the exam room. Put all of this out of your mind as soon as you enter the room. Once you're in the exam, there's no use fretting about those details.

- Positive thinking. This might seem obvious, but thinking positively about the exam and what comes after can be extremely helpful. Some people like to change their mind-set about exams, thinking of it as an opportunity to show off their knowledge, rather than as a painful task that they have to work their way through. Alternatively, focus on what you do know rather than what you don't know, what you can do rather than what you can't do. Once you're in the exam room, there's no point worrying about your weaknesses. Focus on your strengths.

Read Instructions Carefully

This sounds simple, but far too many people trip up on this simple bit of advice. When you enter your exam, the first thing you should do is read the instructions on the front of the question or answer paper. In some cases, an invigilator may read the instructions to you, but feel free to read the instructions before the exam starts.

Answer the Easiest Questions First

This tip is absolutely key for the tougher exams you come across, since it's an excellent way to use your time in the exam hall effectively.

Say you're about to sit your OAR test. You sit down and have the examination instructions read out to you. The invigilator instructs you to start your exam, and then you begin. You open the question booklet to find that the first question seems almost impossible. Before you panic, take a flick through the booklet and look at some of the other questions. If possible, pick the question that looks the easiest to you and start with that.

This is a good technique for two reasons. Firstly, it's a great boost to your confidence when you're feeling unsure about the exam. There's not much worse in an exam than sitting there, becoming more and more demoralised by a question that you don't think you can answer. Starting with more manageable questions will help you ease into the exam, and hopefully you'll recall some information while doing it.

Sometimes, exams can fit together like a puzzle. At first, it seems impossible. But, once you start to put pieces in (answer the questions), the more difficult bits start to make sense. All of a sudden, you're on a roll of answering questions, and then the tough ones don't seem so bad!

The other reason that this is a good technique, is that it represents a good use of your time. There's no point sitting and staring blankly at a question that you can't solve, when there are others that you could be getting on with. Forget about the tough questions for now, bank as many marks you can get with the easier ones, then go back to the hard ones at the end if you have time. This way, you can secure as many marks as possible. In the worst-case scenario, you won't be able to complete the tough questions, but you'll still have earned a few points for all of the others.

Focus on Key Details

Some candidates have a tendency to read a question briefly, then jump straight into their answer without thinking about what's really being asked. For questions which are worth lots of marks, you should take extra care in reading the question fully. If it helps, underline the key parts of the question, so that it's easier to break down.

In mathematical reasoning questions, you'll often be given a large paragraph of text, but only a small portion of it will be relevant to the question that you're trying to answer. Work your way through the paragraph, and highlight or take a mental note of anything that you'll need in order to answer the question.

Double-Check the Question

In a later section, we'll be talking about double-checking answers, but it's just as important to double-check the question that you're answering, before you begin to answer it. Say you're doing a math question:

$$8.93 \times 9.54 = ?$$

Before you start answering the question, take note of everything about it. Where are the decimal points? What operation needs to be performed? Sometimes, people make silly mistakes and misread the question, getting things mixed up.

It's not pleasant finding out that you've answered a question incorrectly just as you get to the end of it, so it pays to look over the question multiple times. In the case of math questions, it might help to re-write the question in the answer box if there's space. This means you can look back at it quickly, without making any mistakes.

Don't Hedge Your Bets

Hedging your bets happens when a candidate tries to give 2 or more answers to a single question, trying to cover as many bases as possible and be less likely to lose marks. After all, if you give lots of different answers, surely one of them is bound to be correct? The problem with this is that examiners will mark harshly against answers like these. Take a look at this example of someone who has tried to hedge their bets:

Question: What part of the human body carries blood back to the heart?

Answer: Veins/Arteries

Only one of the given answers can be correct, since one of them sends blood away from the heart and the other brings blood back to it. The correct answer is "veins", but in this example, both possible answers have been put in. This example answer shows that whoever answered the question wasn't sure, so put both down just in case. Examiners will not award marks for this, so it's essential that you don't try to play it safe in this way. Be confident in your answer.

Avoid Blanking

Have you ever been in a situation where you had something in your head that you were about to say, or about to write, but then completely forgot what it was just before saying or writing it? It can be frustrating in everyday life, but when it happens in an exam it can lead to all kinds of problems. Key details can be forgotten, formulas and tricks may be hard to recall, and sometimes you might just struggle to get off the first page. This is what people refer to as 'blanking'.

Blanking is something that many candidates worry about, and you've likely heard some horror stories about people who have forgotten everything just as they enter the exam. However, it doesn't occur as often as you might think, and it doesn't mean you're going to fail your exam.

The best way to prevent blanking is to keep stress to a minimum. This might be easier said than done, but candidates tend to blank when they haven't had much sleep or have tried to cram their revision into the day before, or the day of the exam itself. This can cause candidates to panic, and while they're busy worrying, anything that might have been holding in their short-term memory gets forgotten. We'll cover stress in more detail later in this chapter.

In addition to keeping stress to a minimum, make sure that you aren't revising on the day of the OAR test, and preferably not the night before, either. In order to retain the information in your revision, you need to commit it to what some people call your 'long-term memory'. It takes time for what you've studied to reach this part of your memory, and things revised in the hours before the exam usually haven't made it there. When revision is being held in the short-term memory, you're generally more likely to forget it, which in turn leads to blanking.

If you find that you've blanked in your exam, here are some tips to keep you calm and help you recover from it as quickly as possible:

Take a few deep breaths before continuing. This is important as you need to stay calm. The more you panic, the less likely you are to remember the information you need. Take a moment to calm down – remember that not performing so well on this exam isn't the end of the world, and that you have the entire paper to remember what you need to know and get back on form.

Look through the question booklet. Sometimes, the wording of a question can jog your memory, or give you a clue of what to write. This can get you started on an answer, which in turn can set off a chain-reaction of memories flooding back, to the point where you remember plenty of information. However, this doesn't always happen; don't rely on this as a replacement for revising over a longer period of time.

Start with an easier question. Some questions require less knowledge than others. If you find yourself blanking in the exam, go onto a question that doesn't need as much precise information as others. Sometimes, a question won't be asking for specific terms or details, but rather an analysis or critical take on the material. These are the questions to do first if you find yourself blanking. This won't work for every kind of exam, however.

Don't attempt any of the larger questions straight away. It might be tempting to just throw caution to the wind and get the toughest or biggest question out of the way. This is usually a bad idea, since these questions contain the most marks. You want to answer these once you've remembered as much as possible, so wait until later in the exam to try them.

Double-Check Your Work

Everyone makes mistakes. It's almost completely unavoidable, even under relaxed conditions, to create a piece of work that's free of any errors at all. In the exam, you're going to feel a bit rushed, and you're probably going to be working very quickly. This is fine, but remember that you're more likely to make mistakes this way. So, it's important that you go back and check everything you've written. Small, silly errors can cost you big marks, so it's vital to make sure you've fixed anything that could be wrong.

Proofreading can take place at two times during your exam. You can either re-read each of your answers individually after you've completed each one, or you can go back at the end of the exam (if you have time) and check every question in one go.

Both have pros and cons, and one method may just suit you better. You might prefer the methodical approach of checking every answer once you've finished it. Alternatively, you might find it easier to handle the exam, knowing that you've answered every question that you can, and then go back and check everything in one go.

How to go about proofreading your work will depend on the subject that you're taking, and the questions that you've been asked. Re-read the question, and make sure that you've answered properly. If you haven't done this, quickly add the extra information in the answer box.

When you double-check your work, you might come across something that you've written, but that you know now is incorrect. In this case, you need to cross it out, so that the person marking your exam knows to ignore these incorrect parts. Put a straight, diagonal line through your work, to indicate any work that you don't want the examiner to look at. Then, all you need to do is replace what you've crossed out with something that's correct.

Bring Some Water and Eat Healthily

Bringing water into an exam room can help you to remain focused, as you're supplying your brain and body with a vital nutrient for proper function. If you're allowed to bring water to your exam, you should absolutely bring a bottle.

Some studies show that candidates who take a bottle of water into their exams and drink it get an average score of 5% higher than students who do not. While this might not actually happen for you, this suggests that having a bottle of water handy can be helpful.

On the same topic, eating healthily (and sensibly!) before your exams can make a big difference. Try and avoid drinking carbonated drinks or eating sugary food before an exam. The sugar rush might make you feel on top of the world when the exam starts, but you could have a crash halfway through, leaving you shattered for the final stretch. Instead, try and have a good breakfast in the morning before your exams. See what works best for you, but eggs and fish (such as smoked salmon) can give you plenty of energy to complete your exams with.

Stay Healthy

No matter what happens in your exam, it's important that you stay healthy. This is a slightly more general point, but it can't be emphasised enough.

First, you need to stay mentally healthy. Remember that there's life after your exam, and so you shouldn't put yourself under unnecessary pressure. Some anxiety is unavoidable, but it's important that you don't let it get out of control. Between study sessions, remember to do things that you enjoy, be it sports, video-games, reading fiction, watching television or spending time with friends or family. This will help you to feel calm during your exam and remind you that there's more to life than your exams.

Secondly, you need to think about your physical wellbeing. While you're busy revising and making yourself ready to ace the exams, it's easy to forget about your own health. While it's good to take revision seriously, you can't neglect your own physical needs, and so you should make sure to get a lot of the following during your exam:

- Sleep. Everyone needs sleep in order to function, and you're no different! Adults need between 8 and 10 hours of sleep per night, so you should be aiming for this as well. A good night's sleep, particularly the night before your exam, can make a world of difference on the day of the test. It will also help you massively during your revision time.

- A balanced diet. This can be easily overlooked, but being fed well can be the key to acing an exam on the day. You want to feel as prepared as possible, so be sure to get a good meal the night before and on the day of your exam. Also, try to eat plenty of fruit and vegetables, since they help strengthen your immune system. Some candidates work themselves extremely hard, then forget to boost their immunity, leading to colds and flu. You want to avoid this – being ill during an exam is horrible!

Avoiding Stress

What is Stress?

Stress is an unpleasant sensation that you feel when you're under too much pressure. It's a common feeling to have as a candidate preparing for an exam, especially when studying for and sitting your exams. The pressure that you feel can sometimes grow to become too much to deal with, and can be bad for your physical and mental health, as well as your exam performance.

Stress can be the result of several different worries about your exam. Worries can include:

- Will I get the grades I want/need?

- Have I revised enough?

- Have I left it too late to start revising?

- What will my family and friends think of me if I don't do well?

- What if bad questions show up in my exam?

- What if I oversleep and miss my exam?

- What if I get into the exam hall and forget everything?

Rest assured that, no matter what you're worried about in the run-up to your exams, thousands of other candidates have felt similar things. It's quite normal to feel a bit stressed during the exam. However, it's important to keep these pressures in check, and prevent stress from harming you or your chances of acing your OAR test. The rest of this section will be devoted to discussing stress, and will hopefully give you some advice on how to manage and prevent it.

How Do I Know if I'm Feeling Exam Stress?

It can be difficult to know if you're stressed or not. Some people are genuinely stressed, but dismiss it as normal – perhaps because they do not know any different. If you're feeling stressed at all, it's important to identify it and make steps against it before stress becomes too much to handle.

The symptoms of stress occur because, when the body is under pressure, it releases hormones which trigger 'fight or flight' responses in the body. In prehistoric times, these symptoms may have proven useful for preparing the body to protect itself from a threat, or be able to run away quickly. Nowadays, we aren't particularly worried about fighting or escaping from wild animals, so the symptoms of stress aren't particularly helpful.

How Can I Prevent Exam Stress?

First of all, remember that stress is completely normal for candidates sitting an exam. This exam is very important, and if you're feeling stressed about them it at least shows that you recognise their significance. While stress definitely isn't a good thing, the bright side of it is that you and your body are aware of how important your OAR test is. Now what's needed is to keep your stress levels down so you can operate at peak performance, and more importantly stay healthy in body and mind!

This section will cover the "dos" and "don'ts" for dealing with exam stress, both during revision and the exam itself.

DO...

Start revision early. This might seem obvious by now, but starting your revision earlier in the year is one of the best ways to avoid stress. The more time you have, the less you need to do each day. This gives you more free time, and also allows you to make use of extra time to do other revision activities such as practice papers.

Listen to your body. At times, you might feel like an unstoppable machine, speeding through revision. During this period, it can be tempting to ignore your bodily needs and soldier on. Likewise, when you're worried about not finishing your revision in time for the exam, it seems like a good idea to stay up all night to make up lost time. Whether you're ignoring your body because you're doing well or poorly, it isn't advisable to do so. You can't function properly without food, water and sleep, so remember to take the breaks in your revision to do these things. That way, when you come back to revising, your study sessions will be more valuable because you're able to focus harder.

Forget about the exam once it's over. It's important not to linger on an exam once you've finished it. As soon as the exam ends, you have permission to forget about it entirely. Try and avoid talking to others about details of the exam, because it might give you second thoughts about what you wrote in yours. There's no use worrying now since there's no way of changing what you've written. Stay confident and move onto the next exam.

Ask others for support. No person is an island, and everyone occasionally needs someone else to help them through tough times. When the going gets tough, don't be afraid to talk to your friends and family. Find people you trust and talk to them about your worries. Sometimes, just talking about things can make you feel calmer, even if you don't figure out any solutions. More often than not, your worries will be amplified by the general worry of exams, and so talking through your problems and rationalising them can be a form of therapy. You might find that your worries are just the result of paranoia, and aren't grounded in reality.

DON'T...

Rely solely on online forums. The internet can be an excellent place to find information and techniques for studying. You have access to plenty of specific advice on a range of subjects, and this can supplement your work in the classroom and your revision at home. However, not all resources are useful, and not all environments on the internet are good for your wellbeing. Some exam-focused chatrooms and forums can do more harm than good. You may come across people who are arrogant about the work that they've done, trying to make you feel worse about your studies as a result. Make use of the internet when it comes to your OAR tests, but try not to linger in places that won't make you feel better about your own studies.

Pay attention to how much revision others are doing. You'll likely find other people in person or online who are all too willing to let you know how much revision they're doing, and how well their revision is going. These people are probably having a really hard time with their revision, and are just looking for a way to feel better about themselves. If you need to, ignore these people until your exam is over, and instead spend your free time with people who don't stress you out as much.

Set goals you can't meet. Always remember that there's only so much that you can do each day when it comes to revision. If you've put together a revision timetable then this shouldn't be a problem, but double-check how much work you've allotted for each day. During the revision period, take note of how much you're doing each day, and adjust your timetable based on this. For example, if you're finding that 10 topics is far too many, try reducing it to 7 or 8. Likewise, if you're able to do loads more than 5, experiment and see how many topics you get through in one day. The aim of this is to finish each day satisfied that you did everything you can, and that everything is completed. This should work towards preventing exam stress.

Rely on caffeine or other stimulants. Caffeine will affect your concentration and sleep-patterns. If you become dependent on it, you'll find yourself unable to perform properly without it, which could lead to uncomfortable and unproductive revision sessions. This could cause stress over time, as you require a certain chemical in your body in order to feel ready to study or sit an exam. In addition, interrupting your sleeping-pattern can make you feel tired during your study time, and can cause stress in general. Do yourself a favour and keep away from the caffeine during the exam.

THE OAR TEST READING COMPREHENSION

Note: This chapter contains passages which contain strong opinions on a range of topics. These opinions do not reflect the beliefs of How2Become Ltd or its employees. These opinions are used to create interesting discussion and drive debate.

The first part of the OAR that you need to study for is the Reading Comprehension test. As the name suggests, this test focuses on your ability to read and comprehend a text, and then answer questions based on what you've read. In this chapter, we'll be taking a look at the general types of reading comprehension question, followed by sample questions for each kind of question that you might face during the OAR test.

What Types of Question are in the Reading Comprehension Test?

The Reading Comprehension test focuses on the following areas:

1. Inferences and Logic.

2. Analysis of Literature.

3. Comprehending Paragraphs.

Let's take a look at each of these in detail.

Inferences and Logic

This type of question tests your ability to read a piece of text, interpret the information within it, and then choose from a list of statements to find the most logical inference based on the text.

When someone infers something, or makes an inference, then they are coming to a conclusion which is based on evidence. Logic (whether inductive or deductive) is applied to this evidence, which in turn brings the individual to their conclusion. When someone makes an inference, they're commonly seen as 'reading between the lines', figuring out a conclusion that isn't explicit, but rather implied from the evidence.

Unlike some of the other types of claim, such as assumptions, inferences are based on evidence. However, inferences aren't always correct, and shouldn't be accepted as truth. While an inference might seem correct, it's entirely possible that it's overlooking other possibilities.

It might be the case that you have plenty of evidence for something, but you completely misconstrue it. All of the evidence going into the inference could be strong, but the way you think about it could be incorrect.

For example, you might come across a police officer talking to an individual in the street. You might infer from the fact that the individual isn't in handcuffs, and that the officer is talking to them, that they witnessed or are reporting a crime. This seems to be a sensible conclusion, but there are other possibilities. The individual might know the police officer personally, and is quickly stopping to say hello to them. Alternatively, they might be asking for directions. So, the inference might be incorrect.

In the critical thinking test, you'll be commenting on how likely the inferences are to be true or false, rather than if they are simply correct or incorrect. This means that you need to think about all of the other possibilities other than the inference in question. Generally speaking, the more possibilities there are, the less likely the inference is to be true.

However, some inferences are better than others. For example, say that you couldn't find your keys and phone. You were sure that you left them on the kitchen table, but now they're gone. You could make several inferences as to how this happened:

1. A burglar snuck into your house undetected and stole them;

2. There was a brief lapse in the laws of the universe and they disappeared into thin air;

3. A ghost took them to play a practical joke on you;

4. Someone else in your house moved them;

5. You are mistaken about where you left your keys and phone, and they're actually somewhere else.

Some of these inferences are more likely than others. For example, you might say that inference 1 is probably false. This is because it could have happened – it isn't impossible – but the chances of it happening are slim. Inferences 2 and 3 are, depending on your perspective, either probably false or certainly false. This is because you might consider both of these things to be impossible.

Inferences 4 and 5 will fall into the category of probably true. This is because they are the most rational explanations for why your keys and phone appear to have moved from the kitchen table. They don't rely on the supernatural or incredibly unlikely (perhaps even impossible) changes to the fabric of the universe. Whatever the case, they're far more likely to occur than the first three inferences. Therefore, it might be safe to say that these inferences are probably true, and the most likely overall.

You also need to pay attention to whether or not the inference contradicts the information in the text. For example, say that the text says that people who frequently use social media are more likely to struggle to make friends in real life. If one of the inferences says that social media users are more likely to have more friends, then there's a contradiction between the two. This means that the inference is either probably false, or certainly false.

How Do I Answer an Inference Question?

Inference questions in the Reading Comprehension test can be tricky because you need to be able to think critically about the information in each question. Here's an example of an inference question:

Scientific studies have discovered a link between chewing gum and better performance when it comes to tests. Researchers believe that this is because the act of chewing gum correlates with heightened activity in the hippocampus – the region of the brain which handles memory. When activity in the hippocampus is increased, it appears as though the ability to recall memories is strengthened.

Inference 1: Chewing gum causes heightened activity in the hippocampus.

Inference 2: There is a correlation between chewing gum and better recollection of memories.

Inference 3: Students who chew gum will perform worse in exams than students who do not.

Inference 4: Scientists have a firm understanding of how chewing gum makes you perform better in tests.

In the OAR test, you'll be expected to find the inference which is true based on the text. So, in the above example, inference 2 is correct: there appears to be a link between chewing gum and heightened test performance. From this, we can *infer* that there is a correlation between the two. Therefore, inference 2 is the correct answer.

To better understand why this is the **correct** answer, let's take a look at why inferences 1, 3, and 4 are **incorrect**.

Inference 1 is an incorrect answer because there is no evidence in the text that shows that chewing gum causes heightened activity in the hippocampus. Rather, the text states that there is a *correlation* between chewing gum and heightened activity in the hippocampus. Therefore, there is no definitive causal relationship between the two, although there might be. However, this still means that inference 1 is not the correct answer.

Inference 3 is also incorrect because it assumes that students who chew gum will perform worse than students who do not. This is incorrect because the text suggests that, in fact, students who chew gum will perform *better*, or at least are more likely to. Therefore, inference 3 is not the correct answer.

Inference 4 is incorrect because the text doesn't provide any reason for believing that scientists have a firm understanding of how chewing gum makes you perform better in your tests. All they have is a hypothesis of how chewing gum might have an impact on behaviour in the hippocampus.

Remember that you might find that some, or even all, of the answer options to make sense. However, only one of the answer options will follow purely from the information in the text. Try to put aside all external knowledge and instead just focus on what's in front of you.

Now that we've taken a look at an inferences question, let's move on to the next type of question you might face: analysis of literature.

Analysis of Literature

Questions in this category test your ability to read a text, analyse the author's writing, and then choose a conclusion which best fits it. Here, you might be asked to analyse the language or tone of the text. For example, the author of the passage might use a specific word. Your task could be to figure out what the impact of that word has on the reader, or why that word was decided on, rather than another.

How Do I Answer an Analysis of Literature Question?

This kind of question can vary immensely. Here are some of the areas you might need to think about when answering an analysis of literature question:

- Style/Genre - The kind of text that the passage takes form as, such as non-fiction, fiction, instructions, and more.

- Tone - Whether the text is light-hearted, humorous, somber, formal, or informal, you need to be ready to take this into account in when reading the passage.

- Language - The question may ask you to explain why the author has used a specific word or phrase.

As you can see, there are three main types of question in the Analysis of Literature category. While they are all different, you can use the following tips to approach them in a similar way:

1. Make sure you read the passage carefully before even starting to look at the answer options. Once you've read it, re-read it with the question in mind.

2. Think carefully about what impact the language, genre, or tone is in the passage. For example, colloquial language might result in a more light-hearted tone, which in turn will have an effect on the reader.

3. Read each of the answer options and decide on which makes the most sense to you. It might be the case that many of the answers seem reasonable. However, you can only choose **one.**

Now, let's take a look at an example question for analysis of literature:

Nick sighed as he drudged his way over to the car. The snow had now settled above his ankles, attempting to entrench his feet with every step. This wouldn't usually be a problem, but Nick had left his boots in the trunk of the car - his sneakers were no match for the weather.

Why does the author use the phrase "attempting to entrench" to describe the snow?

a) To give the impression that the snow is alive and fighting against Nick.

b) To demonstrate how much difficulty Nick is having as he walks through the snow.

c) To show that the snow is spiteful.

d) To make the audience sympathize with the snow.

So, like other questions in the OAR test, you will have to choose from four answer options. In the above example, the correct answer would be:

b) To demonstrate how much difficulty Nick is having as he walks through the snow.

This can be figured out using a process of elimination:

Answer option A is unlikely to be correct because the text does not give the impression that the snow is actually alive and personified. Rather, the author is using creative language to create an image for the main character: Nick. The snow isn't purposefully working against Nick, but it might feel that way to him. This also means that answer option C is incorrect: the snow isn't spiteful, but it might seem that way to Nick. Finally, answer option D is incorrect because the language does not evoke any sympathy for the snow. If anything, the language is prompting the audience to sympathize with Nick.

To truly succeed in an Analysis of Literature question, you need to be able to think creativgly about what the text is trying to do. If you can understand the purpose and the objective of the text, you'll be on the right track to answering questions of this kind.

Comprehending Paragraphs

The final question type that you'll come up against in the Reading Comprehension test requires that you 'comprehend paragraphs'. A question of this kind will provide a passage, and then ask you to figure out its main idea. Generally speaking, this involves being able to identify what the overall point of a passage is, putting aside any less important claims and ideas.

How Do I Answer a Comprehending Paragraphs Question?

This question comes down to how well you can identify the key idea of a passage. While this might seem simple, some passages can be dense with information and ideas, to the point where it's hard to tell which is the most important one. Here are some tips for finding the main idea in a passage:

1. Main ideas tend to run throughout the entire passage, with every point linking back to the main idea in some way. Try looking at all of the other points. What do they have in common? If many of them all connect to the same idea, then that is likely the 'main' idea of the passage.

2. The main idea of a text won't always be explicit. By this, we mean that you might need to read between the lines to find the underlying main idea of a passage.

3. In some cases, the main idea of a text will be the conclusion of the passage. Sometimes, it will be a summary of the entire passage. You can use a process of elimination on the answer options to come to the answer which seems to be the best match.

Now, let's take a look at an example of a comprehending paragraphs question:

Some people argue that the modern world is at its safest and most structured, whilst others believe that society has never been more chaotic. While we have many systems of power, process, and organization, we also have disorder and disharmony. Perhaps it makes more sense to look at our country and society by finding the average between these two extremes, rather than using the extremes to define us.

What is the main idea of the above passage?

a) That the world is inherently chaotic.

b) That the world is inherently ordered.

c) That society sits somewhere in-between its most chaotic and most ordered aspects.

d) That we shouldn't fret about the extremes in society.

So, we now need to look at each of these answer options to figure out which is correct.

Answer options A and B are not the main idea of the passage because they are presented as competing ideas which have equal importance in the passage. Therefore, neither of them can be the main idea on their own.

Answer option C is the correct answer because it's the idea which results from all of the other ideas in the paragraph. The ideas in answer options A and B come together to give us answer option C.

Answer option D is not the correct answer because it is not an idea which is expressed in the passage.

As you can see, finding the main idea of a passage or argument isn't always obvious. We'll now be moving onto some sample questions to give you an opportunity to get a better feel for how to answer Comprehending Paragraphs, Analysis of Literature, and Inferences questions.

Reading Comprehension Sample Questions

Question 1

A swarm of bats whipped and weaved through the trees, an amorphous mass which danced through the forest. Despite the density of the trees, it appeared as though the bats knew exactly where to go. Their wings moved discordantly, creating a cacophony of flapping which betrayed the swarm's otherwise utter unison. Eventually, they settled on a single beech tree, as a blob of black and brown which seemed to fuse with the tree's leaves.

What is the purpose of the language in this passage?

a) To give a description of the forest.

b) To demonstrate that the bats are both united in their movement but also somewhat individualistic.

c) To portray the bats as a group of graceful creatures.

d) To portray bats as sinister.

Answer

Question 2

The October Revolution of 1917 was a turning point in world history. It spelt the end of Russia as a monarchist power, and the beginning of Soviet Russia –the first state to attempt to realize communist ideology, and put it into practise. It all hinged on the success of the October Revolution: a final push by Vladimir Lenin and the Bolshevik Party to overthrow the recently instated Provisional Government. Had this revolution been a failure, it is quite possible that the Soviet Union would never have formed.

What is the main idea of the above passage?

a) That the October Revolution of 1917 was incredibly important.

b) The Bolshevik Party led the October Revolution.

c) Soviet Russia was the first communist state.

d) Soviet Russia is the only communist state.

Answer

Question 3

As he perused the store's shelves, Alex pondered about the quantity of sneakers he would buy if he was rich. 14 pairs was his initial answer: 1 for each day of the week, and then a second pair as a back-up in case he got bored. What if he got bored of the back-ups? He supposed another seven pairs wouldn't hurt. However, then came the issue of storage. Where do you put 21 pairs of shoes? Alex then remembered that, in this hypothetical scenario, he was rich; a mansion with a sneaker closet would be no big deal.

The above passage contains a large number of questions. Which of the following answers best describes their use in the passage?

a) They show Alex's thought process as he ponders in the store.

b) They're rhetorical questions that are supposed to get the reader thinking.

c) They're a gateway into another world where Alex is rich.

d) They're questions that the reader is supposed to answer.

Answer

Question 4

The UK currently encourages its population to eat 5 portions of fruit or vegetables per day in an attempt to stay healthy. Retailers and grocers are allowed to make this part of their marketing, citing the '5-a-day' campaign on their packaging. However, recent health research conducted in the UK suggests that eating 5 portions of fruit or vegetables per day isn't enough for a healthy lifestyle. The studies show that 10 portions of fruit or vegetables per day are necessary to maintain a healthy diet. Currently, it is against the law for packaging on products to be misleading in the UK.

Which of the following is an inference which can be made from the above passage?

a) That not enough people are eating healthily in the UK.

b) That products which have the '5-a-day' campaign on their packaging or in their marketing are more likely to sell.

c) That the UK has better healthy eating policies and campaigns than other countries.

d) That companies will need to change their marketing from '5-a-day' to '10-a-day.'

Answer

Question 5

Technology companies who specialise in handheld devices such as tablets and smartphones should invest in making their products more intuitive for elderly people. This demographic hasn't been tapped into yet and could greatly benefit from such devices. Lots of elderly people could benefit from new technology that would make their lives much more convenient, especially when they might not be as mobile as they used to be.

What is the main idea of the above passage?

a) Elderly people have trouble getting from place to place.

b) Technology companies are performing well.

c) Technology companies need to make more money.

d) Technology companies are missing a demographic by not creating products for elderly people.

Answer

Question 6

A modern 'reboot' of an old science fiction film has released to critical and commercial acclaim. It contained some of the features of the original, but critics were most impressed by the risks it took, and how willing it was to differ from the movie it was based on. Surveys and review aggregate websites found that audiences were also pleased with the movie.

Which of the following is an inference which can be made from the above passage?

a) This film did well commercially because it differed from the original.

b) Audiences love science fiction movies.

c) This film reviewed well because it differed from the original.

d) Science fiction films were experiencing a slump.

Answer

Question 7

There has been a recent spike in personal data of customers and clients leaking in many businesses. Members of congress are now being pressured by constituents to take action against businesses which make use of customer and client data in a way which either does not benefit the customer, or outright impacts them negatively.

What is the main idea of the above passage?

a) Congress will have to make a decision on whether to legislate against data leaks.

b) People are unhappy about businesses leaking data.

c) Data leaks do not benefit the customer.

d) Data is being leaked by businesses.

Answer

Question 8

All doctors must study medicine at university. This takes five years at university, and beyond that training can take up to sixteen years in total to fully qualify. Nicola is 8 years into her training as a doctor. Anyone who takes a break of two years during their studies is required to sit a returning exam to make sure that they have retained the skills and information required to continue their studies. Nicola is about to take the returning exam.

Which of the following is an inference which can be drawn from the above passage?

a) Nicola is no longer fit to be a doctor.

b) Nicola took a two-year break during her studies.

c) It takes all doctors sixteen years to fully qualify.

d) Doctors can train outside of a university.

Answer

Question 9

Mimi sighed audibly as she trudged her way through the grassy, marshy fields. The sky was as drab and uninspiring as her father's journey playlist. Even the trip there was never-ending. Why did her family insist on dragging her to these tragically monotonous events? They didn't even give her a choice, branding her as "anti-social" if she didn't attend every single one.

What is the purpose of the quotation marks around the term "anti-social" in the passage?

a) To make it more significant.

b) As a quotation to demonstrate what people call Mimi.

c) To draw the reader's attention to it.

d) To demonstrate dialogue.

Answer

Question 10

Scientists have found a link between faster reflexes and lower sperm counts in males. Men with faster reflexes tend to have lower sperm counts. People who perform well in video games tend to have fast reflexes. People who have fast reflexes also tend to be quite good at tennis. Aaron is very good at video games.

Which of the following is an inference which can be drawn from the above passage?

a) Having fast reflexes causes a low sperm count.

b) Aaron is more likely to have a lower sperm count than others.

c) Aaron is good at tennis.

d) Being good at video games causes a low sperm count.

Answer

Answers

Question 1

Answer = b) To demonstrate that the bats are both united in their movement but also somewhat individualistic.

Explanation = The language in this passage describes the bats as an amorphous mass, which suggests that they are unified in movement. However, it also describes the movement of their wings as discordant, implying individuality or disharmony.

Question 2

Answer = a) That the October Revolution of 1917 was incredibly important.

Explanation = The passage emphasizes at two different points that the October Revolution was of great importance. Firstly, it states that it was "a turning point in history." In addition, it states that had the revolution not happened, "it is quite possible that the Soviet Union would never have formed."

Question 3

Answer = a) They show Alex's thought process as he ponders in the store.

Explanation = The first sentence states that Alex is pondering. Since Alex answers the questions himself, this means that they probably aren't rhetorical questions. Therefore, answer option A seems to be the most reasonable.

Question 4

Answer = d) That companies will need to change their marketing from '5-a-day' to '10-a-day'.

Explanation = It's stated in the passage that companies use '5-a-day' as part of their packaging, and also that this is no longer accurate for people wishing to live a healthy lifestyle. In addition, it's against the law for packaging to be misleading. Therefore, we can infer that the packaging will need to be changed from '5-a-day' to '10-a-day'.

Question 5

Answer = d) Technology companies are missing a demographic by not creating products for elderly people.

Explanation = All of the points in the paragraph feed into the main idea that technology companies are missing a demographic by not creating products for elderly people.

Question 6

Answer = c) This film reviewed well because it differed from the original.

Explanation = The passage states that critics were impressed by the film's willingness to differ from the original, and it reviewed well. It's highly likely that this is why the film reviewed well.

Question 7

Answer = b) People are unhappy about businesses leaking data.

Explanation = Each of the points in the passage is predicated on complaints from constituents about businesses leaking data.

Question 8

Answer = b) Nicola took a two-year break during her studies.

Explanation = The passage states that Nicola is taking the returning exam, and that anyone who takes a two-year break during their studies must take the exam. Therefore, Nicola must have taken a two-year break in her studies.

Question 9

Answer = b) As a quotation to demonstrate what people call Mimi.

Explanation = In the sentence, it states that "they didn't even give her a choice, branding her as "anti-social". The content of this sentence suggests that this is a quotation attributed to 'they', with 'they' being Mimi's family.

Question 10

Answer = b) Aaron is more likely to have a lower sperm count than others.

Explanation = Aaron is good at video games, and people who are good at video games tend to have fast reflexes. Men who have faster reflexes tend to have lower sperm counts. Therefore, Aaron is more likely to have a lower sperm count than others.

THE OAR TEST
MATHEMATICAL
REASONING

The second test we'll be taking a look at in this book is the Mathematical Reasoning test. Like the Reading Comprehension test, this test is multiple-choice, meaning that you have to choose the correct answer from a list of answer options. This time, however, you'll be figuring out math questions and problems, rather than reading bodies of text and making inferences.

The mathematical reasoning test is 40 minutes long, and you will need to answer 30 questions. This gives you approximately 1 minute and 20 seconds to answer each question, which means you need to work quickly in order to complete the test!

In this chapter, we'll be taking a look at the main types of question that you'll find in the Mathematical Reasoning test, some tips for success in math questions, followed by some sample questions to give you a feel for the OAR Mathematical Reasoning test.

What Do I Need to Know for the Mathematical Reasoning Test?

The Mathematical Reasoning test will include questions in the following areas:

- Order of Operations
- Fractions;
- Decimals;
- Percentages;
- Factors;
- Multiples
- Ratios;
- Algebra;
- Linear equations.

As you can see, this is a significant list of topics. Let's take a look at some explanations for these areas so that you'll know how to answer the questions in the OAR test.

Order of Operations

The order of operations is as follows:

Parentheses ( )

Exponents X^2

Multiplication X

Division ÷

Addition +

Subtraction -

Fractions, Decimals, and Percentages

Fractions, decimals and percentages are all ways of describing **PART** of a whole number.

You can convert between fractions, decimals and percentages, and you need to learn how to do this!

FRACTION	DECIMAL	PERCENTAGE
$1/2$	0.5	50%
$1/4$	0.25	25%
$3/4$	0.75	75%
$1/3$	0.3333...	$33\ 1/3\%$
$2/3$	0.6666...	$66\ 2/3\%$
$1/5$	0.2	20%
$2/5$	0.4	40%
$1/10$	0.1	10%
$2/10$	0.2	20%

Inequalities

INEQUALITY SYMBOLS

>	Greater than.
<	Less than.
≥	Greater than or equal to.
≤	Less than or equal to.

For example:

* 5,000 > 2,000 = 5,000 is GREATER THAN 2,000.

* 300 < 600 = 300 is LESS THAN 600.

Fractions, Decimals, and Percentages

Fractions, decimals and percentages are all ways of describing **PART** of a whole number.

You can convert between fractions, decimals and percentages, and you need to learn how to do this!

FRACTION	DECIMAL	PERCENTAGE
$1/2$	0.5	50%
$1/4$	0.25	25%
$3/4$	0.75	75%
$1/3$	0.3333...	$33 \, 1/3\%$
$2/3$	0.6666...	$66 \, 2/3\%$
$1/5$	0.2	20%
$2/5$	0.4	40%
$1/10$	0.1	10%
$2/10$	0.2	20%

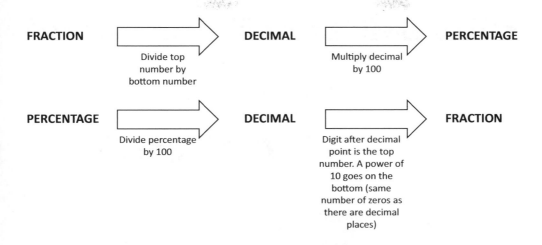

Fractions

$\dfrac{2}{5}$ ➔ The top number is called the NUMERATOR.
➔ The bottom number is called the DENOMINATOR.

THE NUMERATOR

The numerator number tells you how many 'bits' we are <u>trying to work out</u>.

THE DENOMINATOR

The denominator number tells you how many bits there are '<u>altogether</u>'.

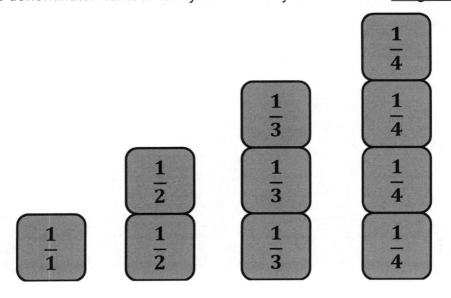

Equivalent Fractions

Equivalent = 'the same as'.

Equivalent fractions look different, but are actually representing the same thing.

$$\frac{1}{2}$$

$$\frac{2}{4}$$

$$\frac{4}{8}$$

Simplifying Fractions

The word **SIMPLIFYING** simply means 'to make it simple'. Sometimes, you can simplify fractions in order to make them easier to understand.

This is similar to finding equivalent fractions. However, instead of multiplying, you will divide – you want to make the fraction smaller!

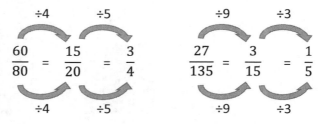

Mixed Fractions

MIXED FRACTIONS have both an integer and a fraction.

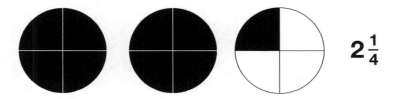

$2\frac{1}{4}$

An IMPROPER FRACTION is where the top number of the fraction is bigger than the bottom number of the fraction.

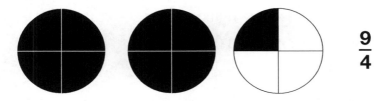

$\frac{9}{4}$

To write a mixed fraction as an improper fraction:	To write an improper fraction as a mixed fraction:
$4\frac{2}{3}$	$\frac{16}{5}$
• Multiply the whole number by the bottom number of the fraction (12). Add the top number of the fraction (12 + 2 = 14). • This number will form the top part of the fraction. • Leave the bottom number of the fraction as it is: $\frac{14}{3}$	• How many 5s go into 16 exactly? Answer = 3 • How many is left over? Answer = 1 • So, 3 is the whole number. • 1 is the top part of the fraction, and the bottom number will be the same: $3\frac{1}{5}$

Adding and Subtracting Fractions

CROSSBOW METHOD: ADDITION

$$\frac{3}{4} + \frac{2}{5} = \frac{15+8}{20} = \frac{23}{20} = 1\frac{3}{20}$$

Draw two diagonal lines through both of the fractions as shown. (This forms the **CROSS** which looks like a multiplication sign).

It tells you to multiply the 3 by 5 = 15
It tells you to multiply the 4 by 2 = 8.

Then draw your **BOW** (from the bottom number of the first fraction to the bottom number of the second fraction).

Again, multiply these two numbers: 4 x 5 = 20

CROSSBOW METHOD: SUBTRACTION

$$\frac{4}{7} - \frac{1}{3} = \frac{12-7}{21} = \frac{5}{21}$$

Draw two diagonal lines through both of the fractions as shown. (This forms the **CROSS** which looks like a multiplication sign).

It tells you to multiply the 4 by 3 = 12
It tells you to multiply the 7 by 1 = 7.
12 - 7 = 5

Then draw your **BOW** (from the bottom number of the first fraction to the bottom number of the second fraction).

Again, multiply these two numbers: 7 x 3 = 21

Multiplying and Dividing Fractions

ARROW METHOD: MULTIPLICATION

$$\frac{5}{9} \times \frac{3}{5} = \frac{15}{45} = \frac{3}{9} = \frac{1}{3}$$

Draw an arrow through the two top numbers and multiply.
5 x 3 = 15

Draw an arrow through the two bottom numbers.
9 x 5 = 45

Done! (Some fractions will be able to be simplified, as shown in the above example).

ARROW METHOD: DIVISION

$$\frac{4}{7} \div \frac{3}{4} = \frac{4}{7} \times \frac{4}{3} = \frac{16}{21}$$

This is actually quite simple. Turn the second fraction upside down. Change the divide sum to a multiply, and then use the **SAME** method as if you were multiplying.

You will get the answer correct every time!

Key thing to remember:

When you are dividing two fractions, don't forget to turn the second fraction **UPSIDE DOWN** before you multiply the numbers.

Work Out a Fraction of a Number

To find a fraction of something:

1) Divide the whole number by the bottom number of the fraction.

2) Then, multiply by the top number of the fraction.

Alternatively:

1) Multiply the whole number by the top number of the fraction.

2) Then, divide the number by the bottom number of the fraction.

EXAMPLE

Work out $\frac{5}{8}$ of $272.

STEP 1

Divide 272 by the bottom number of the fraction (8).

- $272 \div 8 = 34$

STEP 2

Multiply 34 by the top number of the fraction (5).

- $34 \times 5 = \$170$.

So, $\frac{5}{8}$ of $272 is $170.

Decimals

Like fractions, decimals are another way of writing a number that is not whole.

A decimal is in fact 'in-between numbers'.

6.48 ⟶ This is in between the number 6 and the number 7.

USING PLACE VALUES

In order to work out what the decimal is representing, you should use place values.

These include: units, tenths, hundredths and thousandths.

Adding and Subtracting Decimals

0.5 + 0.62

How to work it out:

$$
\begin{array}{r}
0.5 \\
+\ 0.62 \\
\hline
1.12 \\
\end{array}
$$

The decimal points need to be lined up!

Your answer should begin by adding the decimal point in first, and then add up the columns from right to left.

2.46 - 1.35

How to work it out:

$$\begin{array}{r} 2.46 \\ - 1.35 \\ \hline 1.11 \end{array}$$

The decimal points need to be lined up!

Your answer should begin by adding the decimal point in first, and then subtracting the columns from right to left.

Multiplying and Dividing Decimals

2.5 x 0.2

How to work it out:

- Remove the decimal points.

    25 x 2 = 50

- Now add in the decimal points. **REMEMBER**, you need to work out how many numbers come **AFTER** the decimal point in the question.

- You should notice that two numbers come after the decimal point (the .5 and the .2).

- Therefore 2 numbers need to come after the decimal point in the answer.

    25 x 2 = 50

- So the answer would be 0.50 or 0.5. It is usually written as 0.5 (the 0 at the end is not necessary).

REMEMBER: division is easy if you are dividing by whole numbers. You need to move the decimal points in both numbers the same number of places.

5.39 ÷ 1.1

How to work it out:

Move the decimal point 1 space.

53.9 ÷ 11.

- Now ignore the decimal point in 53.9, do long division and then add it in at the end.

```
        049
    11 | 539
      -  0
         0
        53
      - 44
        99
      - 99
         0
```

Put the decimal point in the answer directly above the decimal point in the question.

```
           04.9
ANSWER = 4.9  11 | 53.9
```

Recurring Decimals

A recurring decimal is a decimal that goes on forever. For example, 0.4̇ means 0.444444.....

If two dots are used, this shows the beginning and the end of the recurring numbers. For example 0.6̇13̇ means 0.613613613...

Percentages

Percentages are used to work out part of a number. For example 25% of something is equivalent to $\frac{1}{4}$ or 0.25

Percent ⟶ out of 100

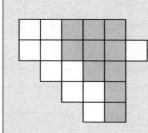

- To work out what percentage of this shape is shaded, you first need to work out the total number of squares.

Total number of squares = 20.

- Now work out the number of squares shaded.

Number of squares shaded = 10.

- There are 20 equal parts which means each square represents 5% (5 x 20 = 100). So, 5% x 10 (shaded squares) = 50%

Find x% of y

To work out the percentage of a number, i.e. 35% of 300, you should **ALWAYS** use the following method, as it guarantees that you get the correct answer.

35% of 300

Step 1 = 300 ÷ 100 = 3

Step 2 = 3 x 35 = 105.

Step 3 = 105 is 35% of 300.

Alternatively, you can convert the percentage into a decimal. So 35% become 0.35 x 300 = 105.

Expressing X as a Percentage of Y

To express a number as a percentage of something else, you will need to divide x by y and then multiply by 100.

For example, write 30¢ as a percentage of $1.20

Step 1

Convert the pounds into pence. You need to work with the same units.

Step 2

Divide 30¢ by 120¢.

30 ÷ 120 = 0.25

Step 3

Multiply this by 100.

0.25 x 100 = 25%

Rounding Up and Rounding Down

When the units are LESS THAN 5, you will round down.

When the units are MORE THAN 5, you will round up.

If the unit IS 5, you will also round up!

There are different ways you could be asked to round a number up or down. This is usually asked by using the words 'to the nearest'.

Sometimes, you will be asked to round a number to a significant figure. This is very similar to rounding to decimal places, except that you will focus on the number.

How to round a number to significant figures:

STEP 1

Identify the number of significant figures you are working with. For example, if you are trying to work out 2 s.f. then you will focus on the **SECOND** digit.

STEP 2

Then, look at the next digit to the right of this number. This is called the **DECIDER**.

- If it's 5 or higher, you will round up.

- If it's 4 or less, you will leave the number as it is.

STEP 3

Once you have rounded the number, you should fill up the gaps to complete the number (zeroes will be needed up to the decimal point).

Factors

Factors are numbers that can be divided **EXACTLY** into other numbers.

Work out the factors of 60.

1 x 60 = 60   4 x 15 = 60

2 x 30 = 60   5 x 12 = 60

3 x 20 = 60   6 x 10 = 60

Multiples

How to find the lowest common multiple (lcm):

Finding the 'common' multiples of numbers means finding a number that they both have in common.

EXAMPLE

Find the lowest common multiple of 2 and 5.

Step 1

Write out the first few multiples of 2.

> 2, 4, 6, 8, 10…

Step 2

Write out the first few multiples of 5.

> 5, 10, 15, 20, 25…

Step 3

Find the lowest multiple that both 2 and 5 have in common.

Step 4

The lowest common multiple for 2 and 5 is 10. (There is no smaller number that is a multiple of 2 and 5, therefore this is the correct answer).

Prime Numbers

Prime numbers are numbers that cannot be divided by anything else apart from the number 1 and itself.
All prime numbers up to 100 have been shaded.

1	2	3	4	5	6	7	8	9	10
11	12	13	14	15	16	17	18	19	20
21	22	23	24	25	26	27	28	29	30
31	32	33	34	35	36	37	38	39	40
41	42	43	44	45	46	47	48	49	50
51	52	53	54	55	56	57	58	59	60
61	62	63	64	65	66	67	68	69	70
71	72	73	74	75	76	77	78	79	80
81	82	83	84	85	86	87	88	89	90
91	92	93	94	95	96	97	98	99	100

Percentage Increase and Percentage Decrease

To work out the percentage increase of a set of data, you need to remember this formula:

PERCENT INCREASE % = DIFFERENCE ÷ ORIGINAL NUMBER X 100

To work out the percentage decrease of a set of data, you need to remember this formula:

PERCENT DECREASE % = DIFFERENCE ÷ ORIGINAL NUMBER X 100

Ratios

Ratios are a way of showing how things are shared.

The process of simplifying is quite easy. All you have to do is find a number that both values of the ratio can be divided by.

The ratio will be in its simplest form, when there are no numbers that can be divided into both values of the ratio.

EXAMPLE

Simplify 40 : 60. Write your answer in its simplest form.

Step 1

Both '40' and '60' can be divided by 10.

- If you divide both numbers by 10, you get the ratio: 4 : 6

Step 2

Both '4' and '6' can be divided by 2.

- If you divide both numbers by 2, you would get the ratio: 2 : 3

Step 3

No other numbers can be divided equally into 2 and 3, so 2 : 3 is the simplest form of 40 : 60.

See how the ratios 40 : 60, 4 : 6 and 2 : 3 are all equivalent ratios = they all mean the same thing!

Algebraic Expressions

When it comes to algebra, letters and/or symbols can be used to represent numbers.

TERM = this is a number or letter on its own.

- x x^2 $8x^3$

EXPRESSION = an expression is when terms are used alongside operations WITHOUT an equals sign.

- $3x - 2$ $xy - x$

EQUATION = an equation is when terms are used alongside operations WITH an equals sign.

- $3x + 4 = 10$

Simplifying Expressions

Simplifying expressions, also known as collecting "like" terms, allows you to make the expression easier to read.

EXAMPLE

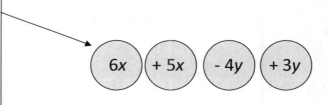

As you can see, the first term does not have an operation shown. However, this means that there is an INVISIBLE + sign.

6x   + 5x   - 4y   + 3y

Using the expression in the above example, you can see that there are two different expressions - the terms that have the letter '**x**', and the terms that have the letter '**y**'.

That means we can simplify the expression as follows:

- The '**x**' terms can be collected together to give $11x$.

- The '**y**' terms can be collected together to give $-1y$.

Expanding Brackets

Multiplying brackets is quite a tricky thing to get your head around.

There are a few things that you can learn to make your life easier when it comes to multiplying out brackets:

1. The most important thing to remember is that everything **INSIDE** the bracket should be multiplied by the term (or number) **OUTSIDE** of the bracket.

2. If there is a minus sign **OUTSIDE** of the bracket, that will **REVERSE** all of the signs when multiplying.

EXAMPLE 1

$$3(a + b) + 2(a + b)$$

- $(3a + 3b) + (2a + 2b)$
- $5a + 5b$

EXAMPLE 2

$$(y - 1)(3y + 4)$$

- $(y \times 3y) + (y \times 4) + (-1 \times 3y) + (-1 \times 4)$
  $\quad$ **$3y^2$** $\qquad$ **+ 4y** $\qquad\quad$ **-3y** $\qquad\qquad$ **-4**
- $3y^2 + 1y - 4$

Factorization

Factorizing is the process of putting brackets back in to expressions.

EXAMPLE

Factorize:

$$4y - 8$$

How to factorize:

- First of all, you need to find the highest common factor. This will either be a number or term.

- The common factor will be placed outside of the bracket. The numbers and terms inside the brackets will be multiplied by the outside term.

4y - 8

- 4 and 8 are both divisible by 4. So, the number 4 will be placed outside of the brackets.

- Next, you need to work out what you need to multiply by the 4 in order to get the rest of the expression.

$$4(y - 2)$$

If you expand this answer, you should reach the expression we first started with: $4y - 8$.

Quadratic Equations

The most general way to write a quadratic equation is like so:

$$ax^2 + bx + c = 0$$

QUADRATIC EQUATIONS contain only terms up to and including x^2. In the above example, you need to remember that a cannot be equal to 0, but the terms b and c can.

QUADRATIC FORMULA

This formula can be used for equations that cannot be factorized. The formula is:

$$\frac{-b \pm \sqrt{b^2 - 4ac}}{2a}$$

EXAMPLE

Solve the following quadratic equation:

$(x + 9)(x - 4) = 0$

- The product of $x + 9 = 0$ OR $x - 4 = 0$.
- $x + 9 = 0$
- $x = -9$
- $x - 4 = 0$
- $x = -4$
- So, $x = -9$ or $x = -4$.

Mathematical Reasoning Sample Questions

Question 1

Representation of the grades students achieved across five subjects

	English	Math	Science	History	Media	Grade	Pass Mark
David	A-	B+	C-	C+	B+	A+	96-100
Billy	C-	C+	B+	A+	A	A	91-95
Elliott	B+	B-	A+	A-	C	A-	86-90
Taralyn	C+	B+	B+	C+	A+	B+	81-85
Alecia	C	C+	A-	B-	C+	B	76-80
James	B-	B+	C-	C+	C	B-	71-75
Gareth	B+	B-	A	B-	C-	C+	65-70
Duncan	B-	C-	C+	C-	C	C	59-64
Joe	B+	B	B	C	A	C-	50-58

In the above table, find the minimum possible of total marks for all nine candidates in Science.

A	B	C	D	E
507	776	667	676	None of these

Question 2

In the above table, what is the highest mark across all five subjects that David could have got?

A	B	C	D	E
298	386	320	408	None of these

Question 3

There are two lists of numbers. One list contains 11 numbers, the average of which is 36. The second list contains 13 numbers and has the average of 41. If the two lists are combined, what is the average of the numbers in the new list? Give your answers to the nearest whole number.

A	B	C	D	E
36	37	38	39	40

Question 4

The diagram below shows the plan of a building site. All angles are right angles.

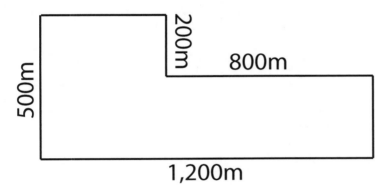

What is the area of the building site? Give your answer in hectares.

1 hectare = 10,000m² = 2.47 acres.

A	B	C	D
60 hectares	40 hectares	44 hectares	4.4 hectares

Question 5

The diagram below shows the layout of an animal sanctuary.

The animal sanctuary contains 6 separate enclosures for different animals.

The animal sanctuary is a rectangle with the following dimensions:

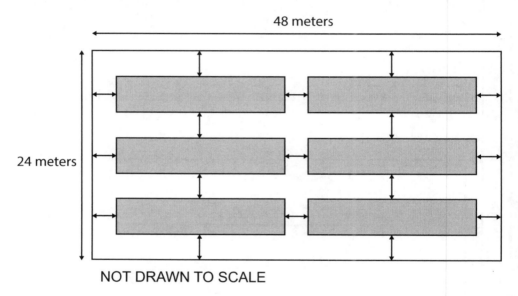

NOT DRAWN TO SCALE

The distance from the outer edge of the sanctuary to the enclosures must be 1.5 meters.

The distance between each enclosure must be 1.5 meters.

Each enclosure is the exact same size. Using the information provided in the diagram above, work out the length and height of an enclosure.

A	B	C	D
Length: 6 meters Height: 21.75 meters	Length: 21.75 meters Height: 6 meters	Length: 24 meters Height: 6 meters	Length: 21.75 meters Height: 24 meters

Question 6

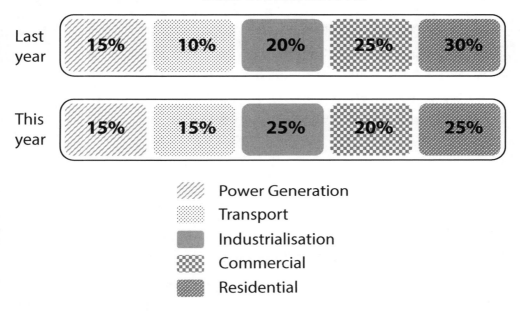

Carbon Emissions

If transport emitted 6 million tons this year, and industrial emissions are the same as last year, what were the commercial emissions last year?

A	B	C	D	E
11.5 million tons	10 million tons	3 million tons	12.5 million tons	8.5 million tons

Question 7

A square field, S, has an area greater than 6400m². Its length is increased by 31m and its width is also increased by 35m to give a rectangular field, R. Which one out of the following is true?

A. Area S > area R and perimeter S > perimeter R

B. Area S = area R and perimeter S = perimeter R

C. Area S < area R and perimeter S < perimeter R

D. Area S < area R and perimeter S > perimeter R

E. Area S > area R and perimeter S = perimeter R

Answer

Question 8

A bank pays 6.8% compound interest per year on an investment of $7,000.

What is the value of the investment after two years? Round your answer to 2 decimal places.

A	B	C	D
$476	$7899	$7984.37	$7985

Question 9

The following table shows the cost of booking holidays from a travel agent for next year.

HOLIDAY PRICES				
Types of Holiday Deals	Turkey	Mexico	America	Spain
All inclusive	$276pp	$720pp	$880pp	$320pp
Half board	$220pp	$640pp	$795pp	$275pp
Self-Catering	$180pp	$550pp	$620pp	$235pp

Work out the difference in cost of booking three all-inclusive holidays to Mexico, for two people, instead of booking one-self-catering holiday to Turkey for five people.

A	B	C	D
$1,250	$3,420	$9,000	$4,500

Question 10

The local police force has put out a tender for electrical equipment and supplies. Below are quotes from 3 suppliers.

Electrical Equipment and Supplies	Supplier 1 Total cost over 2 years ($)	Supplier 2 Total cost over 2 years ($)	Supplier 3 Total cost over 1 years ($)
Basic Services	34,550	36,660	15,450
Electrical Safety Checks	39,550	42,000	20,000
Full Equipment Maintenance	120,850	150,500	60,000

Based on an annual year cost, which supplier offers the best price for electrical safety checks?

A	B	C	D
Supplier 1	Supplier 2	Supplier 3	All the same

Question 11

Study the following graph carefully and answer the questions given below.

This graph shows the distribution of candidates who were enrolled for a fitness course and the candidates (out of those enrolled) who passed the course in different institutes.

Candidates enrolled = 1500

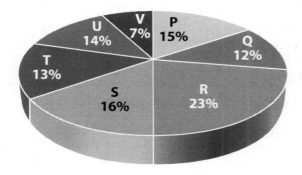

Candidates passed = 920

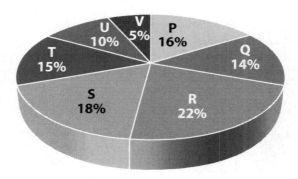

Which institute has the highest percentage of candidates passing the selection process to candidates enrolled?

A	B	C	D
Institute P	Institute Q	Institute T	Institute V

Question 12

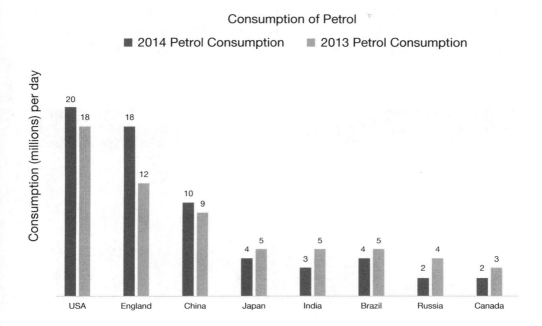

Consumption of Petrol

■ 2014 Petrol Consumption   ▦ 2013 Petrol Consumption

In England, if the petrol consumption per year continued to rise by 6.8% until 2016 and then decreased by 4% from 2016 to 2018, what would be the petrol consumption per day in 2018?

A	B	C	D
18.9 million	19 million	21.5 million	19.8 million

Question 13

The set of data below shows the results in an 11th Grade Media mock exam. The marks are out of 100%. The teacher wants to find the mean mark for this test which was given to 68 pupils. Give your answer to 1 decimal place.

Media mock exam (%)	No. of pupils	No. of pupils X media mock exam (%)
10	0	10 x 0 = 0
20	2	20 x 2 = 40
30	3	
40	6	
50	8	
60	11	
70	8	
80	15	
90	12	
100	3	

A	B	C	D
67%	67.2%	68%	70%

Question 14

Look at the sequence below:

　　1　　9　　17　　25　　33　　…　　…

What are the next two terms in the sequence?

A	B	C	D
42 and 49	44 and 55	40 and 50	41 and 49

Question 15

Factorise:

$$12 + 20x$$

A	B	C	D
(4x + 20)	5(4+5)x	4(3+5x)	4(3x5x)

Question 16

Factorise:

$$x^2 - 81$$

A	B	C	D
(x + 9)(x - 9)	9x+81	9(x+81)	81^2

Question 17

Solve:

$$6(x - 3) = x + 7$$

A	B	C	D
x = 6	x = 7	x = 5	x = 3

Question 18

Simplify:

$$a^2 + a^2$$

A	B	C	D
a^2	$2a^2$	4a	$4a^2$

Queston 19

Factorise completely:

$$20a^2 - 10a$$

A	B	C	D
10a(2a-1)	20a	10a-1	10a

Question 20

The table shows the number of times a die was thrown. It shows how many times each number on the die appeared.

Casts	1	2	3	4	5	6
First 10	2	3	1	1	2	1
First 20	5	4	3	4	3	1
First 30	8	5	6	5	4	2
First 40	10	6	7	6	5	6
First 50	13	7	10	7	6	7

The same number did not appear on any two consecutive casts. If the number 4 appeared in the 20th cast, which number/s could not have appeared in the 11th cast?

A	B	C	D	E
4	1	2 and 3	6	3

Answers

Q1. D = 676

EXPLANATION = 50 + 81 + 96 + 81 + 86 + 50 + 91 + 65 + 76 = 676.

Q2. E = none

EXPLANATION = 90 + 85 + 58 + 70 + 85 = 388. None of the answers match, so therefore the answer must be 'none'.

Q3. D = 39

EXPLANATION = 11 x 36 = 396. 13 x 41 = 533. 533 + 396 = 929 ÷ (11 + 13) = 38.708. To the nearest whole number = 39.

Q4. C = 44 hectares

EXPLANATION = Work out the area of the whole shape: 1200 x 500 = 600,000

Work out the area of the missing rectangle (to make a complete rectangle): 800 x 200 = 160,000

- So, 600,000 – 160,000 = 440,000m².
- 440,000m² in hectares = 440,000 ÷ 10,000 = 44 hectares.

Q5. B = Length of each enclosure = 21.75 meters, Height of each enclosure = 6 meters

EXPLANATION = To work out the length = total 48 meters

- 48 – 1.5 – 1.5 – 1.5 = 43.5
- 43.5 ÷ 2 = 21.75 meters

To work out the height = total 24 meters

- 24 – 1.5 – 1.5 – 1.5 – 1.5 = 18
- 18 ÷ 3 = 6 meters

Q6. D = 12.5 million tons

EXPLANATION = if transport emissions this year are 6 million tons – and equal 15% of the total – the overall total for this year would be 6,000,000 x 100 ÷ 15% = 40,000,000.

So industrial emissions for this year would be = 40,000,000 ÷ 100 x 25 = 10,000,000.

The industrial emissions are the same for last year, so to work out the overall total of last year = 10,000,000 x 100 ÷ 20 = 50,000,000.

So the commercial emissions for last year = 50,000,000 ÷ 100 x 25 = 12,500,000 (12.5 million tons).

Q7. C = Area S < area R and perimeter S < perimeter R

EXPLANATION = if the perimeter is increased on both sides of the Square field S, that means the area of square field R is going to be bigger. This is also true about the perimeter; if both sides are increased in size to form field R, which means the perimeter for R is going to be bigger than that of perimeter S. So, the correct way to demonstrate this is answer C.

Q8. C = $7984.37

EXPLANATION = for this question, it is vitally important to remember that interest will be added on to previous interest.

Step 1 = for the first year = 7,000 ÷ 100 x 6.8 = $476.

- So, 7,000 + 476 = 7,476.

Step 2 = for the second year = 7,476 ÷ 100 x 6.8 = 508.368.

- So, 7,476 + 508.37 = $7,984.368. Rounded to 2 d.p. is $7,984.37

Q9. B = $3,420

EXPLANATION = Self-catering holiday to Turkey for 5 people = 180 x 5 = 900.

All-inclusive holiday to Mexico for 2 people = 720 x 2 = 1440. Booked three times = 1440 x 3 = 4320.

- So, 4320 − 900 = 3,420.

Q10. A = Supplier 1

EXPLANATION = Supplier 1 = 39,550 ÷ 2 = 19775

Supplier 2 = 42,000 ÷ 2 = 21,000

Supplier 3 = 20,000

Therefore, Supplier 1 offers the best price for electrical safety checks, for one year.

Q11. B = Institute Q

EXPLANATION =

$$P = \left[\left(\frac{16\% \text{ of } 920}{15\% \text{ of } 1500}\right) \times 100\right]\% = \left[\frac{16 \times 920}{15 \times 1500} \times 100\right]\% = 65.42\%.$$

$$Q = \left[\left(\frac{14\% \text{ of } 920}{12\% \text{ of } 1500}\right) \times 100\right]\% = 71.56\%.$$

$$R = \left[\left(\frac{22\% \text{ of } 920}{23\% \text{ of } 1500}\right) \times 100\right]\% = 58.67\%.$$

$$S = \left[\left(\frac{18\% \text{ of } 920}{16\% \text{ of } 1500}\right) \times 100\right]\% = 69\%.$$

$$T = \left[\left(\frac{15\% \text{ of } 920}{13\% \text{ of } 1500}\right) \times 100\right]\% = 70.77\%.$$

$$U = \left[\left(\frac{10\% \text{ of } 920}{14\% \text{ of } 1500}\right) \times 100\right]\% = 43.81\%.$$

$$V = \left[\left(\frac{5\% \text{ of } 920}{7\% \text{ of } 1500}\right) \times 100\right]\% = 43.81\%.$$

So, the institute with the highest percentage rate of candidates passed, to candidates enrolled, is Institute Q.

Q12. A = 18.9 million

EXPLANATION = first, you need to work out the percentage increase each year from 2014 to 2016.

So, in 2014 there is 18 (million); to work out a 6.8% increase would equal 106.8%. So, 18 ÷ 100 x 106.8 = 19.2 (million). This is the consumption for 2015. From 2015 to 2016, the same thing applies. 19.2 ÷ 100 x 106.8% = 20.5 (million).

From 2016 to 2017, there is a 4% decrease. So, 20.5 ÷ 100 x 96% = 19.7 (million). From 2017 to 2018 = 19.7 ÷ 100 x 96% = 18.9 (million).

Q13. B = 67.2%

EXPLANATION = Add up the "number of pupils multiplied by media mock exam" and then divide it by the "number of pupils".

Media mock exam (%)	No. of pupils	No. of pupils X media mock exam (%)
10	0	10 x 0 = 0
20	2	20 x 2 = 40
30	3	30 x 3 =90
40	6	40 x 6 = 240
50	8	50 x 8 = 400
60	11	60 x 11 = 660
70	8	70 x 8 = 560
80	15	80 x 15 = 1200
90	12	90 x 12 = 1080
100	3	100 x 3 = 300
Totals		

So, 4570 ÷ 68 = 67.2%.

Q14. D = 41 and 49

EXPLANATION = The number sequence is adding 8 to the previous number.

Q15. C = 4 (3 + 5x)

Q16. A = (x + 9) (x – 9)

Q17. C = x = 5
- 6x - 18 = x + 7
- 5x - 18 = 7
- 5x = 25
- x = 5

Q18. B = 2a²
- a + a = 2a
- Both of these are being squared, so 2a squared = 2a².

Q19. A = 10a (2a – 1)
- Highest common factor = 10
- 10a (2a – 1)
- = 20a² - 10a

Q20. D = 6

EXPLANATION = the question may seem tricky at first, but if you notice, the individual number of 6 was cast once in the first 10 attempts, and only once in the first 20 attempts. Therefore, the number 6 could not have turned up from casts 11 – 20.

THE OAR TEST
MECHANICAL
COMPREHENSION

The final of the three tests we'll be taking a look at is the Mechanical Comprehension test. This test assesses your ability to understand and answer Mechanical Comprehension problems: problems which require a grasp on concepts in mechanics such as gravity and force.

The Mechanical Comprehension test is 15 minutes long, and you must answer 30 questions. This means that you have 30 seconds to complete each question. This is a significant task, so you'll have to work extremely quickly in order to complete the test. However, you must remember to work accurately as well as quickly - it's better to answer half the test accurately than all of the test inaccurately!

Let's begin by taking a look at how to answer mechanical comprehension questions.

Pulleys

If the pulley is fixed, then the force required is equal to the weight. A simple way to work out how to calculate the force that is required, is to divide the weight by the number of sections of rope supporting it.

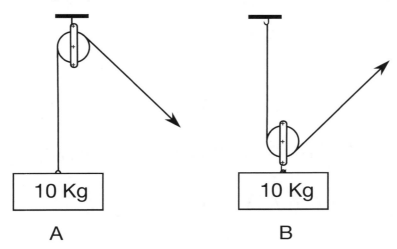

A   B

DIAGRAM A = there is only one section of rope supporting the weight, therefore this can be worked out by = 10 ÷ 1 = 10.

DIAGRAM B = there are two ropes supporting the weight, therefore this can be worked out by: 10 (weight) ÷ 2 (number of ropes supporting the weight) = 5.

Springs

When springs are arranged in a series, each spring can be the subject of the force applied. If the springs are arranged in a parallel line, the force is divided equally between them.

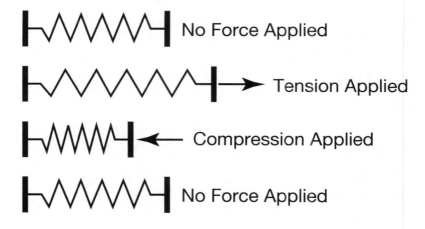

No Force Applied

Tension Applied

Compression Applied

No Force Applied

Gears

If gears are connected by a chain or belt, then the gears will all move in the same direction.

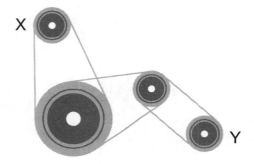

If the gears are touching (as shown in the example below), then adjacent gears move in the opposite direction. In the example, X and Y will move in opposite directions.

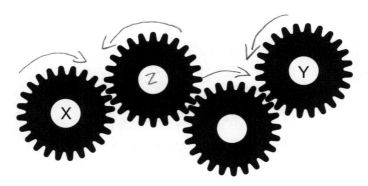

Circuits

Questions regarding circuits usually follow a similar circuit, which will include: a power source, switches, bulbs and a path of wiring.

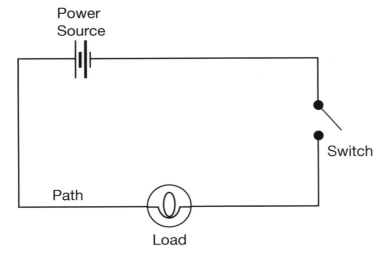

Striking Tools

Sledge	A sledgehammer is a large, flat, often metal head, attached to a handle. It is used to break rock.
Hammer	A hammer is a tool with a heavy metal head used for driving in nails and breaking things.
Mallet	A mallet can be made from metal, plastic, wood, rubber or rawhide. This is used to strike another tool or surface without damaging it.

Fastening Tools

Allen Wrench	A tool to drive bolts and screws with hexagonal sockets in their heads.
Box Wrench	A wrench with a closed socket that covers over a nut or bolt head.
Cutting Pliers	A tool used to cut material such as wire.
Curved-Nose Pliers	A tool used to cut and hold material. Used to bend, re-position, or snip.
Long-Nosed Pliers	A tool used to cut and hold material. Used to bend, re-position, or snip. Longer nose makes them better for snipping.
Offset Screwdriver	A screwdriver with a blade at a right angle to the shaft.
Open-End Wrench	A wrench with jaws having a fixed width of opening at one or both ends.
Phillips Screwdriver	A screwdriver that has a cross-shaped tip.
Pipe Wrench	A tool used for turning soft pipes and fittings with a rounded surface.
Pliers	Pincers used for gripping or bending wire.
Slip-Joint Pliers	Pliers with a pivot point that can be altered to increase the size range of the jaws.
Socket Wrench	A ratchet tool with a series of detachable sockets for tightening and loosening nuts.
Standard Screwdriver	A tool used for turning a screw. This type of screwdriver will have a long, flat head.
Stapler	A device used for fastening objects together with the use of staples.
Torque Wrench	A tool used for setting and adjusting the tightness of nuts and bolts.
Wrench	A tool used to turn something.
Wrench Pliers	A tool with serrated jaws that clamp objects.

Cutting Tools

Bolt Cutters	When the handles are closed, the shears are able to slice through metal objects.
Circle Snips	Circle snips are used to cut curves.
Coping Saw	Coping saws are a type of handsaw that is used to cut shapes or curved lines.
Crosscut Saw	Crosscut saws are a type of handsaw that cuts against the grain of wood.
Hacksaw	A hacksaw is used to cut metal.
Pipe Cutters / Tube Cutters	This is a type of cutter that is used to score and cut metal objects.
Ripsaw	A ripsaw is a type of handsaw that cuts against the grain of wood.
Snips and Shears	Snips and shears have cutting blades (like scissors) which can be used to cut curved or straight.

Chisels

Metal-Cutting Chisels	Chisels that are able to cut into metal. Usually struck with a mallet.
Wood-Cutting Chisels	Chisels that are able to cut into wood. Socket chisels are struck with a mallet to cut through wood. Other chisels require only pressure from your hands.

Drills

Auger Bits	Auger bits pierce large holes.
Countersink	Countersink is a drill which enlarges the surface of a hole so a screw can be inserted.
Twist Drills	Twist drills are used to create holes.

Clamping Tools

Bench Vise	A vise with large jaws which holds material in place.
Clamps	Used when a vise doesn't work. Clamps generally connect to the items (not on a bench)
Handscrew Vise	A vise with two jaws connected by screws. The screws are used to tighten the vise together.
Pipe Vise	A vise that holds round pipes or trims.
Pliers	Pliers can be used to hold objects.
Vises	Hold material while being sawed, drilled or glued.

Finishing Tools

Double-Cut	Double cut files are used for rough work.
Flat Files and Half-Round	Files that are used for general purposes.
Single-Cut	Files that are used for finishing work and sharpening blades.
Square and Round	Files fit square and/or round openings.

Measuring Tools

Calipers	Calipers are used for very small and exact measurements.
Depth Gauges	Depth gauges measure the depths of holes.
Tape Rules	Tape rules are used to measure material.
Level	Levels are a tool which allows you to place it on a surface to see if the surface is level.
Square Level	A square level is used to check the accuracy of an angle.
Thickness Gauges	Thickness gauges measure the thickness of holes.
Wire Gauges	Wire gauges measure the thickness of wire.

Fastening Bits

Bolts	Bolts are flat ended and are held in place by a nut and washer.
Brads and Finishing Nails	These type of nails have heads which are made to fit in line or slighly below the surface of wood.
Common Nails	These are nails that are used for general purposes.
Double-Headed Nails	This type of nail has two heads, one lower than the other. The nail is driven into an object until it reaches the lower head, but can be pulled out by the higher head.
Lag Screws	Lag screws have square or hexagonal shaped heads.
Machine Screws	Machine screws are used for metal. They come in various sizes and have a variety of different heads.
Nuts	Nuts can come in different shapes. They can be square or hexagonal. Cap nuts are round and smooth. Stop nuts prevent screws or bolts from coming loose. Wing nuts have 'wings' on each side so they can be tightened by hand.
Rivets	Rivets are used to fasten metal objects together.
Washers	Washers prevent damage to a surface by preventing the bolt from digging into the materia.
Wood Screws	Wood screws are used to fasten wood objects together.

Electrical Terminology

ALTERNATING CURRENT	An alternating current (AC) is a current that is continuously changing direction.
AMMETER	An ammeter is an electrical unit that measures current. An ammeter needs to be connected in series.
BATTERY	A battery supplies the electrical charge of a circuit. A battery contains more than one cell (see cell for definition)
BUZZER	A buzzer is a transducer which converts energy into sound.
CAPACITOR	A capacitor stores the electrical charge of the circuit. It can be used alongside a resistor in a 'timing' circuit. It acts as a sort of 'filter', whereby it blocks direct current (DC) signals, but permits alternating current (AC) signals from running through the circuit.
CELL	A cell is the component of a circuit that supplies the electrical charge. The larger terminal of the symbol represents the positive element and the smaller terminal represents the negative element. More than one cell = battery.

flash
cards.

CLOSED SWITCH	A closed switch allows a current to flow through a circuit. This is done by closing the switch, which is what you would call an 'on switch', (i.e. it has the power to turn the circuit 'on').
CONDUCTOR	An electrical conductor is anything or any material which can carry an electrical current. Other conductors may conduct heat.
DIODE	A diode is an electrical device that only permits current flow in one direction.
DIRECT CURRENT	A direct current can be established if the current flows in one direction. For example, batteries and solar cells supply direct currents, with a typical battery supplying 1.5 V.
ELECTRON	A subatomic particle that carries the smallest of magnitudes of negative electricity.
FUSE	A fuse acts as a 'safety device' for electrical circuits. The fuse will blow i.e. melt, if the current flowing through the circuit exceeds a specified amount.
HEATER	A heater is a transducer that converts electrical energy into heat.
INDUCTOR	An inductor is an output device which includes a coil of wire that subsequently creates a magnetic field when a current passes through. It can often be used as a transducer to convert electrical energy into mechanical energy by this idea of 'pulling on something'.
INSULATOR	An insulator is a material which acts as a very poor conductor of electricity. Electrical wires are often covered with an insulating material in order to guard the circuit's electrical supply and provide a safety precaution to people using them.
LAMP	A lamp, or a bulb, is used as a transducer which converts the electrical energy within a circuit to permit light. This is often used within cars to indicate a warning light on the dashboard.
LIGHT DEPENDENT RESISTOR	A light dependent resistor, or a photoresistor, is a light-controlled variable. They change resistance as the light level changes.
LIGHT EMITTING DIODE	Often abbreviated as LED, light emitting diode is a transducer which converts energy into light.
OHMMETER	Ohmmeter is a unit that measures resistance.
OHM'S LAW	Ohm's law states that the current in a circuit between two points is directly proportional to the voltage and inversely proportional to resistance.

OPEN SWITCH	An open switch prevents a current to flow through the circuit.
RESISTOR	A resistor is a term that is quite self-explanatory. It restricts the flow of the current. For example, a resistor can be used to restrict the flow of current in an LED.
THERMISTOR	A thermistor is an input device relating to sensors. It is a transducer which converts temperature and heat, into resistance i.e. an electrical property.
TRANSFORMER	A transformer is a type of power supply. It contains two coils of wiring which is linked by an iron core. They are used to increase or decrease alternating current (AC) voltages. The transformer transfers energy through magnetic fields, not electrical fields.
VARIABLE RESISTOR	A variable resistor is used to control the current flow. This type of resistor contains 2 contacts. The resistor permits the control of adjusting lamp brightness and motoring speed.
VOLTMETER	A voltmeter is an electrical unit that measures voltage. This is also known as 'potential difference'.

Electrical Symbols

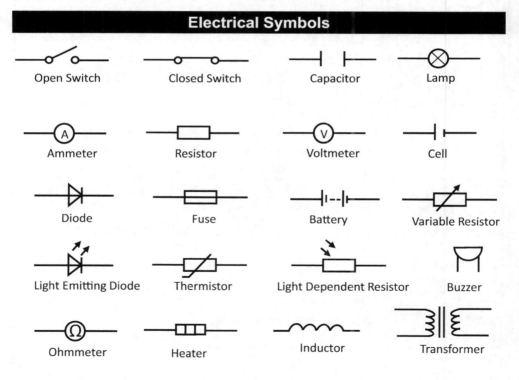

Open Switch	Closed Switch	Capacitor	Lamp
Ammeter	Resistor	Voltmeter	Cell
Diode	Fuse	Battery	Variable Resistor
Light Emitting Diode	Thermistor	Light Dependent Resistor	Buzzer
Ohmmeter	Heater	Inductor	Transformer

Electrical Calculations

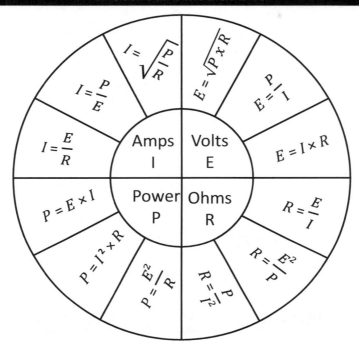

Atoms and Particles

Everything is made up of atoms. Atoms comprise of three particles:

- Protons;
- Neutrons;
- Electrons.

Neutrons – neutral.

Protons and electrons – electrically charged. Protons are positive, and electrons are negative.

The number of protons in an atom is called its 'atomic number'. The total number of electrons in an atom is the same number of the total number of protons in the nucleus. This means that atoms have no overall electrical charge. The nucleus is part of the atom that the particles surround.

Electrical Hazards

Electricity is a form of energy. You need to be fully aware of the dangers involved when using electrical components.

Below is a list of examples of ways in which you can be electrocuted if you are not careful when handling electricity:

- Pushing objects into plug sockets;
- Water touching an electrical compliance;
- Damaged wiring;
- Incorrect wiring;
- Overheated cables and plug sockets;
- Frayed cables.

Currents

AC Electricity

Alternating currents (AC) can be defined through the changes in direction which the flow of electricity undertakes.

DC Electricity

Direct currents (DC) can be established if the current flows in one direction. For example, batteries and solar cells supply direct currents, with a typical battery supplying 1.5V.

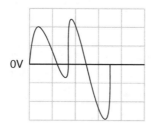

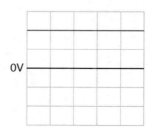

Voltages

Voltage is also known as the potential difference or electromotive force (e.m.f.). The potential difference is needed to make an electrical current flow through an electrical component. For example, cells and batteries are often used to provide the potential difference needed in a circuit.

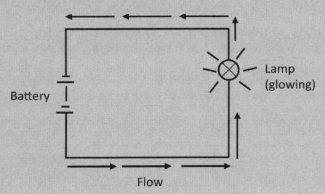

Flow

In the above electrical circuit, you will notice that there is only one source of potential difference (the battery). There is also only one source of resistance (the lamp).

Resistance

The term resistance refers to an electrical element that measures its opposition to a current. A resistance to the flow of electricity in a circuit occurs in most conductors.

The resistance of a wire can be increased in two ways:

- Increasing the length of the wire;
- Decreasing the thickness of the wire.

The resistance of a long wire is greater than the resistance of a short wire. This is because the electrons collide more with ions as it passes through.

The resistance in a thin wire is greater than that of the resistance of a thick wire. This is because a thin wire has fewer electrons to carry the current flow.

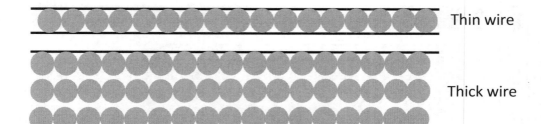

Thin wire

Thick wire

Ohm's Law

Ohm's law is often used to analyse the electrical components within a circuit. In simple terms, Ohm's law specifically focuses on three electrical concepts:

- Potential difference (voltage);
- Current;
- Resistance.

The resistance of an electrical outlet can be found by measuring the current flow and the potential difference, i.e. the voltage running through it.

There is a simple equation to use in order to work out the relationship between current, resistance and potential difference.

REMEMBER the following equation:

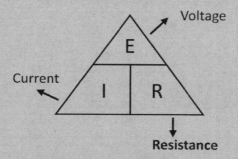

To work out the resistance, eliminate the 'R' from the equation:

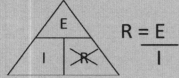

$$R = \frac{E}{I}$$

To work out the current, eliminate the 'I' from the equation:

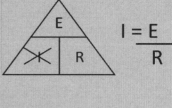

$$I = \frac{E}{R}$$

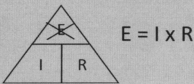

$$E = I \times R$$

Resistance Tolerance

In order to work out the minimum and maximum resistance tolerable of a resistor, you would need to use the following method:

EXAMPLE

What are the minimum and maximum acceptable values if a resistor has the resistance of 20 kΩ and can tolerate ±20%?

Minimum value

Step 1 – 20,000 ÷ 100 x 20 = 4,000.

Step 2 – 20,000 – 4,000 = 16,000Ω or 16 kΩ

Maximum value

Step 1 – 20,000 ÷ 100 x 20 = 4,000.

Step 2 – 20,000 + 4,000 = 24,000Ω or 24 kΩ

Mechanical Comprehension Test - Sample Questions

Question 1

In the following cog and belt system, which cog will rotate the most number of times in an hour?

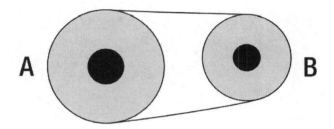

A	B	C
Cog A	Cog B	All the same

Question 2

In the following cog and belt system, which cog will rotate the least number of times in thirty minutes?

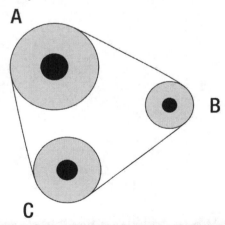

A	B	C
Cog A	Cog B	Both the same

Question 3

Which rope would require the most effort to pull the mast over?

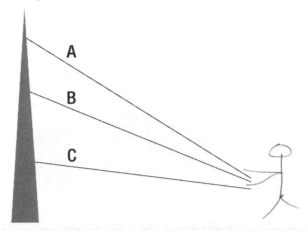

A	B	C
Rope A	Rope B	Rope C

Question 4

If cog A turns anti-clockwise as indicated, which way will cog C turn?

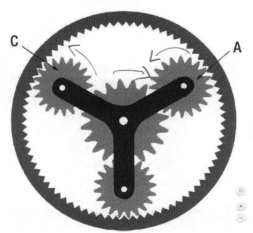

A	B	C
Clockwise	Anti-clockwise	Backwards and forwards

Question 5

What will happen to the air resistance on a car as the car picks up speed?

A	B	C
The air resistance will increase	The air resistance will decrease	The air resistance will stay the same

Question 6

If wheel B moves clockwise at a speed of 20 rpm, how will wheel D move and at what speed?

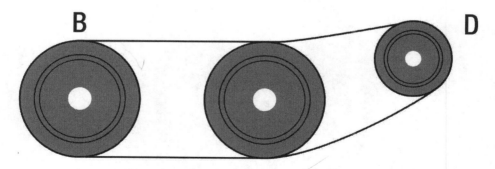

A	B	C	D
Clockwise, more rpm	Clockwise, less rpm	Anti-clockwise, more rpm	Anti-clockwise, less rpm

Question 7

Which is the best tool to use for breaking up concrete?

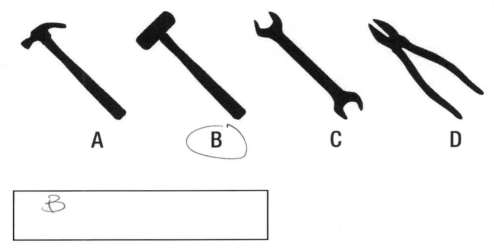

A   B   C   D

B

Question 8

In the following circuit, if switch A closes and switch B remains open, what will happen?

A. Bulbs X, Y and Z will illuminate.

B. Bulb X will illuminate.

C. Bulbs Y and Z will illuminate.

D. No bulbs will illuminate. *open*

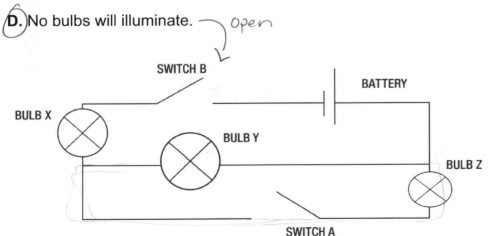

Question 9

In the following circuit, if switch A closes, what will happen?

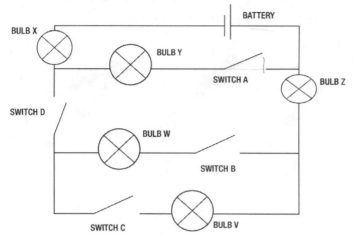

A. Bulbs V, W, X, Y and Z will illuminate.

B. Bulbs X and Y will illuminate.

C. Bulbs X, Y and Z will illuminate.

D. No bulbs will illuminate.

Question 10

Which of the following equations would you use to work out the voltage?

A. Voltage = current ÷ resistance

B. Voltage = resistance ÷ current

C. Voltage = current x resistance

D. Voltage = power x resistance

Question 11

You are looking at the following objects side-on. Which is most unstable and likely to topple first?

If you think they are all the same, then please choose F for your answer.

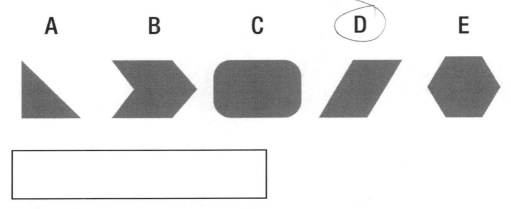

A   B   C   D   E

Question 12

How much weight will need to be placed at point X in order to balance out the beam?

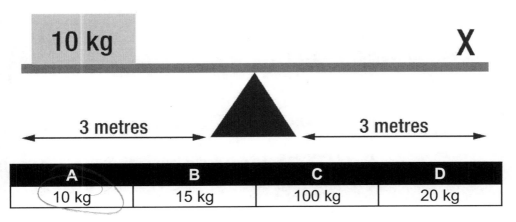

A	B	C	D
10 kg	15 kg	100 kg	20 kg

Question 13

If bar A moves to the left, which way will bar B move?

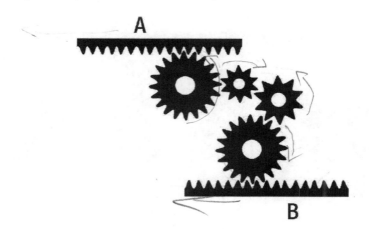

A	B	C
Left	Right	It won't move

Question 14

On the following weighing scales, which is the heaviest load?

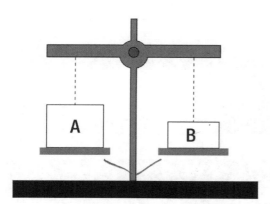

A	B	C
Load A	Load B	Both the same

Question 15

At which point should pressurised air enter the cylinder in order to force the piston downwards?

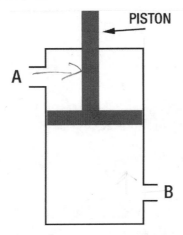

A	B	C
Point A	Point B	Both Point A and Point B

Question 16

In the following nut and bolt configuration, what will happen to the bolt if you turn the nut clockwise?

A. The nut will move upwards.

B. The nut will move downwards.

Question 17

A ball is rolling down a hill. At which point will the ball be travelling the fastest?

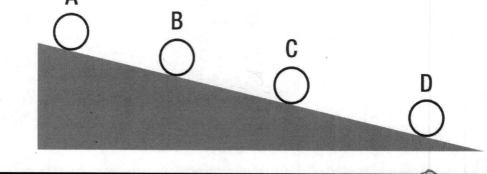

A	B	C	D
Point A	Point B	Point C	Point D

Question 18

Will the bulb illuminate?

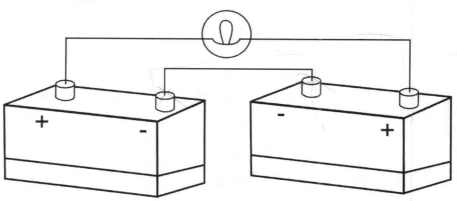

A. Yes

 B. No

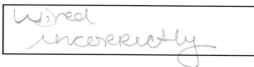
wired
incorrectly

Question 19

At which point will the beam most likely balance?

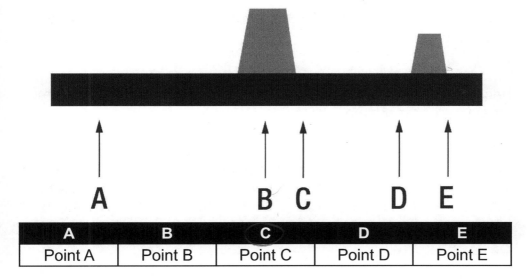

A	B	C	D	E
Point A	Point B	Point C	Point D	Point E

Question 20

Which is the heaviest load?

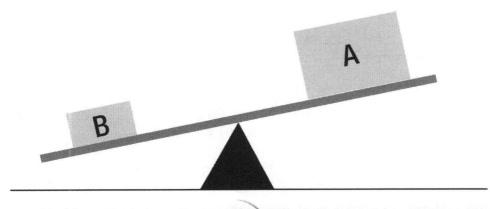

A	B	C
Load A	Load B	Both the same

Answers

Q1. B

Cog B is smaller and therefore will rotate more times in the given timeframe.

Q2. A

Because cog A is the largest of the three cogs it will rotate fewer times for any given timeframe.

Q3. C

The higher up the mast the rope is secured, the easier it will be to pull it over. This is because there is more leverage than a rope secured towards the bottom of the mast. Therefore, rope C will require the most effort.

Q4. B

Cog C will rotate anti-clockwise.

Q5. A

As the car picks up speed, the air resistance will increase.

Q6. A

Wheel D will rotate clockwise, but because it is smaller in size it will rotate more rpm than B.

Q7. B

Both A and B are suitable for breaking up concrete, however, B (sledge hammer) is designed specifically for this purpose.

Q8. D

Because the second switch is still open, the circuit will remain broken and therefore no bulbs will illuminate.

Q9. B

Only bulbs X and Y can illuminate in this circuit because the remaining switches remain open.

Q10. C

In order to work out the voltage, you must multiply the current of the circuit by the resistance.

Q11. D

Out of the objects, D is the most unstable and likely to topple first.

Q12. A

10 Kg must be placed at point X in order to balance the beam.

Q13. A

Bar B will also move to the left.

Q14. C

Both loads weigh the same because the scales are evenly balanced.

Q15. A

Air will need to be forced in at A in order for the piston to move downwards.

Q16. A

The nut will move upwards.

Q17. D

At point D the ball will have gained the most velocity and will therefore be travelling the fastest.

Q18. B

The bulb will not illuminate because the battery is wired incorrectly. For it to illuminate, the positive (+) connection should be connected to the negative (-) connection on each battery.

Q19. C

At point C the beam will most likely balance. You need to place the fulcrum the right amount of distance to balance out the difference in weight.

Q20. B

Load B is the heaviest as the beam is weighing down to the left.

THE OAR TEST - MOCK TEST 1

Now that we've taken a look at the three tests in the OAR assessment, you're ready to begin with your mock tests. Within each mock test, you will find a test for each of the three assessment areas: Reading Comprehension, Mathematical Comprehension, and Mechanical Comprehension.

We recommend that you complete the mock test in a single sitting to give yourself the best simulation of the real OAR test. The time limits for each test are as follows:

•   Reading Comprehension Test - 30 minutes.

•   Mathematical Comprehension Test - 40 minutes.

•   Mechanical Comprehension Test - 15 minutes.

Once you've completed the three sections, head over to the answers to find out where you've performed well, and where you need to improve. If you're struggling, take a moment to return to the sample questions in this book, read their explanations, and then try to attempt the mock test questions again. The content of the explanations should give you some guidance on how to answer questions of the same kind in the future.

Let's start with the first section of the mock test: Reading Comprehension.

OAR Mock Test 1 - Reading Comprehension Test

You have 30 minutes to answer the following 20 questions.

Question 1

Jackson jerked upright from his nap as Gina dumped a pile of letters on his desk. "'Fan' mail, it looks like," Gina smirked, "make sure you reply to all of them by the end of the week." Jackson gazed wearily at Gina as she left the room before proceeding to open the first letter. White envelope, regular size – yet the contents could not have been any more unusual. Jackson turned his heart to stone before working his way through the rest of the pile.

From the language used in the passage, what is most likely contained within the letters?

a) Fan mail.

b) Hate mail.

c) Bills.

d) Court summons.

Answer

Question 2

In 2015, surveys suggested that the number of polyamorous relationships in the USA had risen by 15% since the previous survey in 2014, meaning that there were approximately 30 million adults in the USA participating in polyamorous relationships. However, the number of monogamous relationships had also increased by 20%.

Which of the following is an inference made by the above passage?

a) In general, more people were in relationships in 2015 than in 2014.

b) The rise in polyamorous relationships is causing a decline in monogamous relationships.

c) People like polyamorous relationships.

d) Polyamorous relationships are a threat to modern society.

Answer

Question 3

Jeff found the car at the side of the road at 6am. He then drove it to the nearest gas station and filled the tank with gas. Then, he drove off, never to be seen again. This is why cars should be fitted with tracking devices.

What is the main idea of the above passage?

a) The car had a petrol engine and not a diesel engine.

b) The car wasn't fitted with a tracking device.

c) A tracking device would've stopped Jeff from stealing the car.

d) Tracking devices are expensive.

Answer

Question 4

In 2013, tax avoidance in the USA reached the highest it has been in 25 years. According to the statistics, most of this avoidance occurs in the higher tax brackets. Tax in these brackets is higher than it has been in at least the last ten years.

Which of the following is an inference made by the above passage?

a) People are avoiding tax because they are being taxed too heavily in those brackets.

b) The number of people avoiding tax will continue to rise.

c) There are people avoiding tax in lower tax brackets as well.

d) Tax avoidance is an essential part of society.

Answer

Question 5

It had been three weeks since Martin had boarded the cruise liner, and he still wasn't used to it. He had assumed that the sea sickness would wear off after a few days, and that he'd get used to it. Swaying, rocking, swaying, rocking – this was all he could think about while performing his daily duties as an entertainer onboard the boat. Thankfully, the boat would be making landfall the following weekend.

What is the purpose of the phrase "swaying, rocking, swaying, rocking" in the passage?

a) To give the reader an idea of what it's like being on a boat.

b) To draw the reader's attention away from the details of the passage.

c) To remind the reader that Martin is on a boat.

d) To reinforce Martin's feeling of sea sickness.

Answer

Question 6

The current government has promised to lower taxes for the working class if they are re-elected. However, historical record shows that this very rarely happens. This government says that they will defy this historical precedent. Why should we believe them?

What is the main idea of the above passage?

a) Historically, governments do not help ordinary working people.

b) The current government wishes to break the mold and help working people.

c) Governments like to keep secrets from us.

d) The government will always betray us.

Answer

Question 7

There was no way that Adrienne was going into school today. She had failed all of her tests two weeks ago and couldn't bear to face the rest of the class. It was unfair, Adrienne thought, since she was way smarter than everyone else in the school. The tests were just rigged against her way of thinking about the world.

What is the purpose of the phrase "way smarter" in the passage?

a) The informal tone and grammatically dubious phrase demonstrates that Adrienne is not necessarily 'book smart'.

b) The show that Adrienne is 'cool'.

c) To demonstrate how the school doesn't understand Adrienne.

d) To show that Adrienne is different to her classmates.

Answer

Question 8

Jenny and Mike had been on the road for twelve hours now, with barely even a stop for food. Due to Mike's broken ankle, Jenny had to drive for the entire journey. "Don't worry, honey," Mike mumbled as he looked out of the passenger window. "Once we get to Ohio, you can head down to the beach and relax." Jenny shook her head and chuckled, "There are no beaches in Ohio, you idiot. It's nowhere near the ocean." Mike's eyes glazed over as it dawned on him that he not be able to go surfing once he got to Ohio.

Which of the following does the author suggest in the above passage, through use of language?

a) That Jenny is intelligent.

b) That Mike is not very smart.

c) That they've got a long journey ahead of them.

d) That Jenny is bored.

Answer

Question 9

The amount of organized crime in major cities has been increasing year on year. The number of armed police officers has also increased year on year. The government is now debating spending money on a new specialised taskforce for organized crime. A number of ex-chiefs of police have commented positively on this. We should implement this as soon as possible.

What is the main idea of the above passage?

a) That ex-chiefs of police like the idea of a new taskforce.

b) That organized crime is on the rise.

c) That petty crime is at an all-time low.

d) That a new taskforce should be put in place to tackle organized crime.

Answer

Question 10

Jonathan was already awake when his alarm sounded. The heat in his room was unbearable, someone must have had lit a furnace beneath the floorboards. A film of sweat clung all over his body, making him look like a slightly molten waxwork. He could see cracks of light coming through the closed curtains. He unstuck himself from his bedsheets, and slowly made his way towards the door. A thousand degrees of heat battered him as he approached, and the metal handle was so hot it scalded his hand.

Which of the following does not suggest that Jonathan's room was too hot?

a) The sweat all over his body.

b) The fact that he was already awake before his alarm went off.

c) The use of hyperbole: "a thousand degrees of heat"

d) The cracks of light coming through the curtains.

Answer

Question 11

Changes to United States immigration policy have been in the spotlight for the past two years. While the country never had truly open borders, many have argued that immigrating to the USA was too easy and resulted in an influx of undesirable immigrants from places such as South America, Africa, and Asia. This means that many Americans, but not all, have welcomed stricter immigration policies.

Which of the following is an inference which can be drawn from the above argument?

a) The USA's borders had been open until now.

b) Immigrants only come from South America, Africa, and Asia.

c) Some Americans do not like these new immigration policies.

d) These changes to immigration policy have had a positive impact.

Answer

Question 12

Foreign aid has always been a contentious topic in politics. Many argue that a country should look out for itself before distributing wealth and aid to other countries that need it. Many Americans believe that far too much money is spent on foreign aid, and that it should instead be spent on immigration control, healthcare, or military intervention. However, this assumes that the budget for foreign aid is substantial. In fact, the USA spends less than 1% of its total budget on foreign aid each year.

Which of the following is an inference made by the above passage?

a) That foreign aid is a waste of money.

b) That many people are mistaken about how much is spent on foreign aid.

c) That foreign aid is an essential expenditure.

d) That not enough is being spent on foreign aid.

Answer

Question 13

Erica was going on vacation for the first time in two years, and that time had definitely dragged. Day after day after day of work, followed by stressful weekends of tidying and running errands, had finally worn her down. There had been no respite for Erica until now, as she packed her bags to head away to Spain for three weeks. While she was out there, she planned to do nothing at all but lounge by the pool.

What is the purpose of the phrase "Day after day after day" in the passage?

a) The use of repetition demonstrates how the past two years have dragged on for Erica.

b) It demonstrates Erica's excitement to go on holiday.

c) Erica is tripping over her own words due to the boredom of the past two years.

d) The phrase has no literary purpose in the passage.

Answer

Question 14

Out of all the major businesses in New York, 90% of them disclose their diversity statistics in an annual report. The rest of the firms are being pressured by investors who believe that a greater focus on diversity would increase annual profit.

What is the inference that can be drawn from the above passage?

a) That more diversity equals more money.

b) That diversity is extremely low in these businesses.

c) That all of these businesses practice diversity policies in employment.

d) That investors stand to benefit from firms disclosing their diversity statistics.

Answer

Question 15

A scientific study has found a link between drinking natural spring water and increased performance in the workplace – particularly in office jobs. These researchers are recommending that businesses invest in supplies of bottled spring water to provide to staff if they want to improve productivity.

What is the inference that can be drawn from the above passage?

a) Bottled non-spring water reduces productivity.

b) There is a correlation between drinking spring water and increased performance in the workplace.

c) Drinking spring water will make you more efficient in the workplace.

d) Drinking spring water will make you more efficient in everyday life.

Answer

Question 16

Officer Taylor was on her usual patrol on Tuesday, September 19th, when she came across an unusual sight. She found a large number of homeless people seeking refuge inside the local shopping mall, suggesting that someone had managed to break in somehow. Officer Taylor patrolled the perimeter of the mall to find a point of entry, discovering a window which had been smashed with a car. Officer Taylor was sceptical that any of the homeless persons owned a car, and proceeded to investigate whether that too had been broken into.

What does the formal tone of this passage suggest about the genre of the passage?

a) That it's a police report of some kind.

b) That it contains classified information.

c) That it's a letter of complaint.

d) That it's a historical document.

Answer

Question 17

Tourism research suggests that the Royal Family generates approximately $800 million in tourism per year. Tourism in general generates approximately $5 billion per year. On the years where there is a special occasion such as the Olympics or a football match, this number can increase by a further 60%. In particular, locations such as Buckingham Palace and Westminster Abbey see the most tourists.

Which of the following is an inference which can be drawn from the above passage?

a) The UK makes more money from tourism than the USA.

b) People only go to the UK to see the Royal Family.

c) People are more likely to visit the UK for tourism reasons if royalty exists there.

d) If the Royal Family were to abdicate, the UK would still generate a lot of money through tourism.

Answer

Question 18

There's no explanation for this increase in sales other than the good publicity the company's been getting. This means that we can raise our budget and expand as a company during the next fiscal year.

What is the main idea of the above passage?

a) That the company can't figure out how it's making money.

b) That the company is making a lot of money.

c) That all publicity is good publicity.

d) That the company can expand.

Answer

Question 19

In an interview, a famous actor said she believed that the US government has an obligation to do more for refugees fleeing from areas of crisis. The current government has made no concerted effort to help refugees beyond the bare minimum. This actor says that aiding refugees is one of her top priorities. In response, a number of activist groups have rallied and are trying to bring more attention to the refugee crisis.

Which of the following is an inference which can be drawn from the above passage?

a) This actor will not be voting for the party currently in power in the upcoming election.

b) The opposition has said that they will help refugees if their party is elected.

c) The current government is ignoring the refugee problem.

d) This actor is having an impact on what people believe about the refugee crisis.

Answer

Question 20

In 2007, the number of people buying MP3 players skyrocketed, which in turn popularised the MP3 file format. In 2017, MP3 players are significantly less popular, which some assume is due to the rise in popularity of streaming services. Streaming services do not require this type of file. In 2008, Ryan developed a piece of software which allowed people who bought it to convert audio files to MP3. Now, he's going to have to cease development of it.

What is the main idea in the above passage?

a) Ryan is having to cease development of his software.

b) It's possible to convert audio files to MP3 from other formats.

c) MP3 is on the decline, possibly due to the rise of streaming services.

d) MP3 used to be a popular file format.

Answer

OAR Mock Test 1 - Mathematical Comprehension Test

You have 40 minutes to answer the following 30 questions.

Question 1

A charity arranges a bike race. 120 people take part. $\frac{1}{3}$ of the people finish the race in under half an hour. How many people did not finish the race in under half an hour?

A	B	C	D
40	80	20	60

Question 2

What is $\frac{3}{5}$ of 700?

A	B	C	D
600	450	350	420

Question 3

There are 4,000 millilitres of water contained in the jug. If 1 litre is equivalent to 1,000 millilitres, how many litres of water are there?

A	B	C	D
0.4	0.04	40	4

Question 4

What is the missing angle?

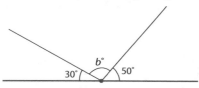

A	B	C	D
120	90	100	140

Question 5

What is 120 multiplied by 13?

A	B	C	D
1,560	1,500	1,320	1,220

Question 6

Find 60% of $45.

A	B	C	D
$22	$27	$33	$35

Question 7

How many lines of symmetry does this shape have?

A	B	C	D
0	1	2	4

Question 8

A packet of biscuits weighs 120 g. Find the weight of 9 packets of biscuits.

A	B	C	D
1080 kg	1880 g	1080 g	108 kg

Question 9

A square field has a perimeter of 72cm. What is the area of the square field?

A	B	C	D
720cm	324cm²	72cm²	160cm²

Question 10

What is $^{24}/_{48}$ in its simplest form?

A	B	C	D
$^{3}/_{6}$	$^{6}/_{12}$	$^{12}/_{24}$	$^{1}/_{2}$

Question 11

Look carefully for the pattern, and then choose which pair of numbers comes next.

5   7   9   11   13   15   17 ...   ...

A	B	C	D
18, 19	19, 21	19, 20	21, 23

Question 12

Look carefully for the pattern, and then choose which pair of numbers comes next.

0   1   1   2   3   5   8   ...   ...

A	B	C	D
12, 18	13, 21	15, 23	13, 22

Question 13

Liz has $12.00. Steph has $8.50.

What is the ratio of Liz's money to Steph's money, in its simplest form?

A	B	C	D
18:12	6:4.25	12:8.5	24:17

Question 14

A newspaper includes 16 pages of sport and 8 pages of TV. What is the ratio of sport to TV? Give your answer in its simplest form.

A	B	C	D
8:16	2:1	4:2	16:8

Question 15

Multiply 6 by 7 and then divide by 3.

A	B	C	D
14	42	12	16

Question 16

Divide 120 by 4 and then multiply it by 5.

A	B	C	D
20	160	150	25

Question 17

What is $^9/_{11}$ of 88?

A	B	C	D
56	81	64	72

Question 18

An English class of 28 have just sat a mock Exam. The exam has 2 sections – Literature and Language. It takes approximately 6 minutes to mark the Literature section and 7 minutes to mark the Language section. Another 2 minutes is given on each exam to check the work again. How long in hours and minutes does it take to mark the English mock exam?

A	B	C	D
6 hours and 45 minutes	5 hours and 25 minutes	7 hours	9 hours and 10 minutes

Question 19

What is 0.9 as a percentage?

A	B	C	D
0.009%	0.9%	9%	90%

Question 20

Simplify $x + 8x - 3x$.

A	B	C	D
$5x$	$6x$	$7x$	$12x$

Question 21

Using the rule of PEMDAS, work out $23.7 - 2.5 \times 8$.

A	B	C	D
3.7	4.2	4.5	7

Question 22

There are 20 buttons in a bag. 12 are red, 5 are green and the rest are white. A button is chosen at random. Work out the probability that it is white.

A	B	C	D
15/20	12/20	3/20	5/20

Question 23

On a school trip at least 1 teacher is needed for every 8 students. Work out the minimum number of teachers needed for 138 students.

A	B	C	D
12	15	18	20

Question 24

Translate the triangle so that point A moves to point B. Draw your translation on the graph.

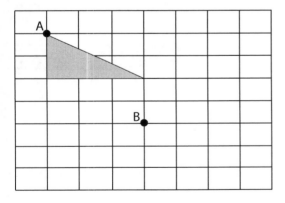

Question 25

Rotate the triangle 90° clockwise so that point A moves to point B. Draw your rotation on the graph.

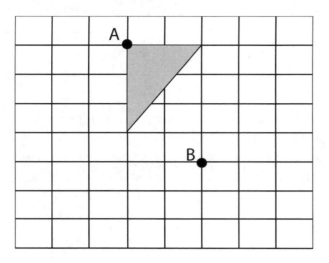

Question 26

The school day starts at 08:45. They have 15 minutes form time and then a 25 minute assembly before the first lesson starts. What time does the first lesson start?

A	B	C	D
09:25	9:15	9:10	9:00

Question 27

A cinema has 27 rows of seats, 28 seats in each row. Tickets are $8 each.

The cinema has sold tickets for every seat apart from 5. Estimate how much, to the nearest hundred, the cinema will make, based on the information provided.

A	B	C	D
$8,000	$6,000	$7,000	$8,500

Question 28

How many grams are there in 2.5 kilograms?

A	B	C	D
0.0025g	250g	2005g	2500g

Question 29

What is the value of 9 in 5.92?

A	B	C	D
9/10	1/9	1/90	9/100

Question 30

The scatter graph shows the number of driving lessons and the number of tests taken to pass by 10 people.

What percentage of the 10 people passed on their first test?

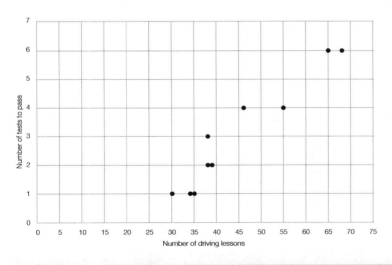

A	B	C	D
20%	15%	30%	35%

OAR Mock Test 1 - Mechanical Comprehension

You have 15 minutes to answer the following 30 questions.

Question 1

Which weight requires the most force to lift it?

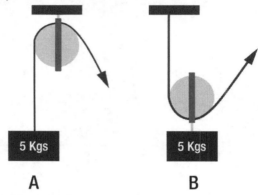

A	B	C
Both the same	Weight A	Weight B

Question 2

How much weight is required to balance point X?

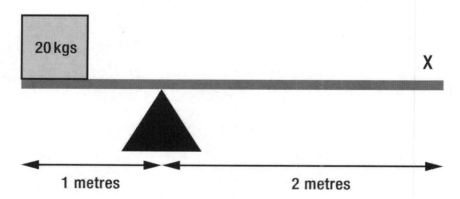

A	B	C	D
5 kg	10 kg	15 kg	20 kg

Question 3

If cog C turns anti-clockwise at a speed of 10 rpm, which way, and at what speed, will cog B turn?

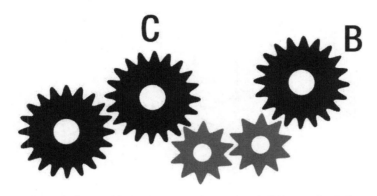

A	B	C	D
10 rpm / anti-clockwise	10 rpm / clockwise	20 rpm / anti-clockwise	20 rpm / clockwise

Question 4

Which tool would you use to claw nails from wood?

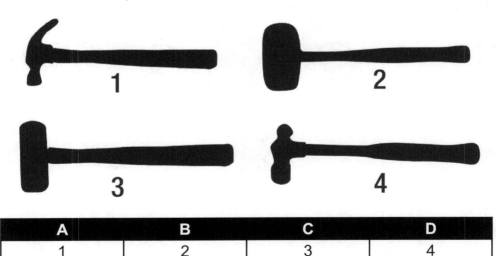

A	B	C	D
1	2	3	4

Question 5

If bulb 2 is removed, how many bulbs will illuminate?

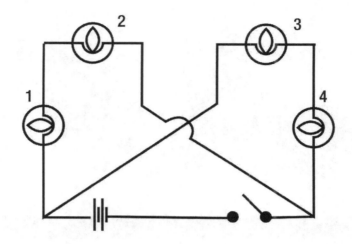

A	B	C	D
1	3	4	None

Question 6

When the switch is closed, how many bulbs will illuminate when bulb 3 is removed, and replaced with cable?

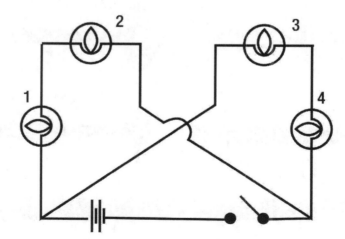

A	B	C	D
None	One	Two	Three

Question 7

If cog B turns anti-clockwise, which way will cog A turn?

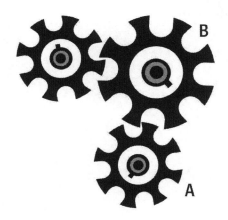

A. Clockwise

B. Anti-clockwise

Question 8

If wheel A is three times the diameter of wheel B and it rotates at 55 rpm, what speed will wheel B rotate at?

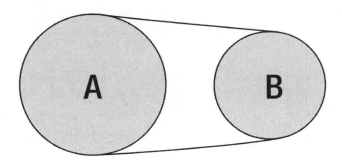

A	B	C
55 rpm	110 rpm	165 rpm

Question 9

How much force is required to lift the 75 kg weight?

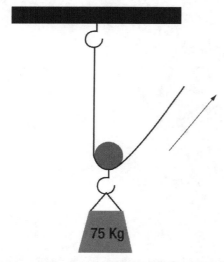

A	B	C	D
25 kgs	37.5 kgs	75 kgs	150 kgs

Question 10

A screw has 8 threads per inch. How many full turns are required for the nut to travel 3 inches?

A	B	C	D
8 turns	12 turns	16 turns	24 turns

Question 11

Cog A has 12 teeth and Cog B has 18 teeth. If cog B completes two full turns, how many rotations will cog A complete?

A	B	C	D
3 rotations	2 rotations	1.5 rotations	1 rotation

Question 12

Two cars are travelling in opposite directions. One of the cars is travelling at a speed of 45 m/s and the other car is travelling at a speed of 30 m/s.

What is their relative speed?

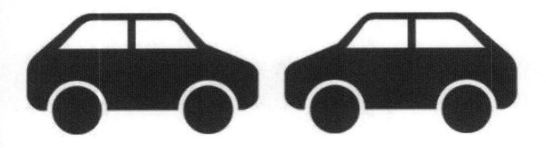

A	B	C	D
60 m/s	45 m/s	30 m/s	75 m/s

Question 13

A thick block of wood rests on an even and level surface. What mechanical principle makes it more difficult to push this block sideways if the surface is made of sandpaper than if it is made of glass?

A	B	C	D
Spring Force	Gravitational Force	Air Resistance Force	Frictional Force

Question 14

Why does an astronaut weigh less on the Moon than on Earth?

A	B	C
The force of gravity is weaker on the Moon.	The force of gravity is weaker on Earth.	The Moon has no gravity.

Question 15

The following three HGVs are parked on an incline. Their centre of gravity is identified by a dot. Which of the three HGVs is least likely to fall over?

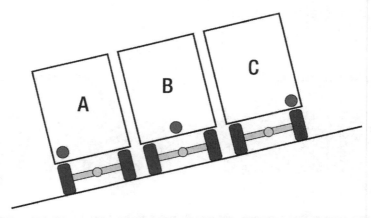

A	B	C
A	B	C

Question 16

Which of the following most resembles a lever?

A	B	C	D
Swing	Car	Elevator	Seesaw

Question 17

To balance the beam, how much weight should be placed on the right-hand side?

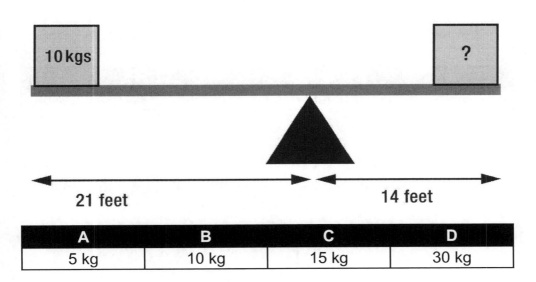

A	B	C	D
5 kg	10 kg	15 kg	30 kg

Question 18

How far from the balance point should the 30 kg weight be placed to balance the beam?

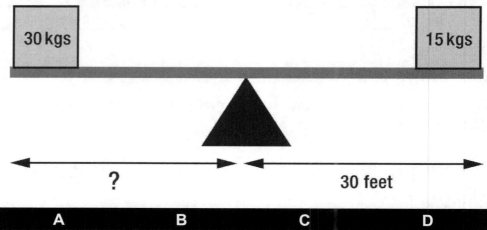

A	B	C	D
5 feet	10 feet	15 feet	45 feet

Question 19

How far would you have to pull the rope up to lift the weight 5 feet?

A	B	C	D
5 feet	10 feet	15 feet	30 feet

Question 20

Friction is an example of what?

A. A contact force

B. A non-contact force

C. Both a contact and a non-contact force.

```

```

Question 21

A block and tackle refers to a device which is used to:

A. Place under the wheel of a car to stop it from rolling backwards.

B. Catch large fish.

C. Leverage a stationary object.

D. Hoist an object upwards by means of rope and pulleys.

```

```

Question 22

Which man is carrying less weight?

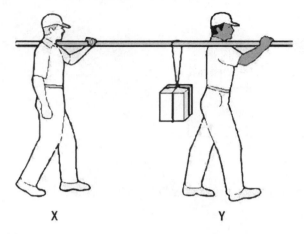

X   Y

A. Man X

B. Man Y

Question 23

If wheel A rotates clockwise, which of the other wheels will also rotate clockwise?

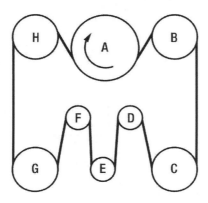

A. All of them

B. B, C, E, G and H

C. D and F

D. D, E and F

Question 24

A builder is told to pitch his ladder a third of the working height away from the building below. How many metres away from the building should the foot of the ladder be placed?

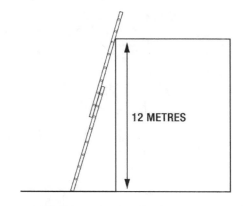

12 METRES

A	B	C	D
36 metres	12 metres	4 metres	3 metres

Question 25

If the object on the left side of the scale is 32 ft. away from the balance point, i.e. the fulcrum, and a force is applied 8 ft. from the fulcrum on the right side, what is the mechanical advantage?

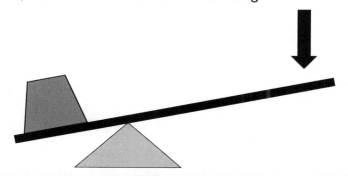

A	B	C	D
4	4.5	18	36

Question 26

A hot air balloon is able to float because:

A. The hot air is turbo-charged

B. The hot air is less dense than the external air

C. The hot air is denser than the external air

D. It is filled with helium.

Question 27

Which of the following materials will float on water?

A	B	C	D
Balsa Wood	Concrete	Coins	Anchor

Question 28

Water is flowing into the following tank through the left-hand side inlet pipe at a rate of 18 litres per minute. If the water is flowing out through the lower right-hand side outlet pipe at a rate of 14 litres per minute, approximately how much time will it take for the tank to overflow?

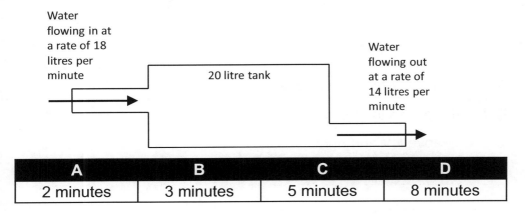

A	B	C	D
2 minutes	3 minutes	5 minutes	8 minutes

Question 29

How much weight will need to be placed on the right-hand side to balance the beam?

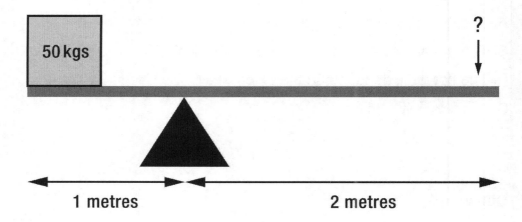

A	B	C	D
100 kgs	200 kgs	50 kgs	25 kgs

Question 30

If the wheel rotates anticlockwise, what will happen to X?

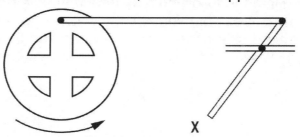

A. It will move to the right and stop.

B. It will move to the left and stop.

C. It will move left and right.

OAR MOCK TEST 1 - ANSWERS

Note: This chapter contains passages which contain strong opinions on a range of topics. These opinions do not reflect the beliefs of How2Become Ltd or its employees. These opinions are used to create interesting discussion and drive debate.

OAR Mock Test 1 Answers - Reading Comprehension Test

Question 1

Answer = b) Hate mail.

Explanation = The use of language in the passage suggests that Jackson has received hate mail. Firstly, Gina smirks as she tells Jackson that he's received 'fan mail', which implies sarcasm. On top of this, the passage uses figurative language to state that "Jackson turned his heart to stone", implying that he had to toughen up to withstand the hate mail he was receiving.

Question 2

Answer = a) In general, more people were in relationships in 2015 than in 2014.

Explanation = The number of both polyamorous and monogamous relationships has increased. Since these are the main two kinds of intimate relationship, it's extremely likely that the number of people in relationships has increased.

Question 3

Answer = c) A tracking device would've stopped Jeff from stealing the car.

Explanation = In the passage, the argument is being made that, had the car been fitted with a tracking device, Jeff would not have stolen the car.

Question 4

Answer = c) There are people avoiding tax in lower tax brackets as well.

Explanation = The passage says that 'most' of this tax avoidance is occurring in the higher tax brackets. This means that people in lower tax brackets are avoiding tax as well.

Question 5

Answer = d) To reinforce Martin's feeling of sea sickness.

Explanation = This is the correct answer because the author uses repetition to give a feeling of what the ship probably feels like for Martin. It reinforces how it's completely occupying his mind as the same rocking and swaying happens constantly.

Question 6

Answer = b) The current government wishes to break the mold and help working people.

Explanation = The question at the end of the passage asks us to question the claim being made by the government in the passage.

Question 7

Answer = a) The informal tone and grammatically dubious phrase demonstrates that Adrienne is not necessarily 'book smart'.

Explanation = The phrase 'way smarter' is not grammatically correct. This plays into the fact that Adrienne performed poorly in her tests, which in turn implies that Adrienne is not conventionally smart.

Question 8

Answer = b) That Mike is not very smart.

Explanation = This is the correct answer for the following reasons. Firstly, Mike didn't realise that there were no beaches in Ohio, suggesting that he didn't really know where Ohio was placed geographically. In addition, it was only after this information appeared that he realised he wouldn't be able to go surfing – he wouldn't have been able to anyway due to his broken ankle.

Question 9

Answer = d) That a new taskforce should be put in place to tackle organized crime.

Explanation = Answer option A is a side-note supporting the creation of an organized crime taskforce. Answer option B is a single sentence introducing the need for an organized crime taskforce. Answer option C is not present in the passage. Therefore, answer option D is the main idea of the passage.

Question 10

Answer = d) The cracks of light coming through the curtains.

Explanation = Each of the other statements or phrases suggest something about the temperature of the room. Jonathan is covered in sweat due to the heat, it has presumably kept him awake during the night, and the exaggerated hyperbole of "a thousand degrees of heat" suggest that it's far too hot for him to cope. This leaves answer option D, which does not really suggest anything about the temperature of the room.

Question 11

Answer = c) Some Americans do not like these new immigration policies.

Explanation = The final sentences states "many Americans, but not all, have welcomed stricter immigration policies." From "but not all", we can infer that there are some Americans who do not like the new immigration policies.

Question 12

Answer = b) That many people are mistaken about how much is spent on foreign aid.

Explanation = The passage states that many people are agitated by the huge amount spent on foreign aid. However, it receives a miniscule amount of money from the overall budget. Therefore, we can infer that many people are mistaken about how much is spent on foreign aid.

Question 13

Answer = a) The use of repetition demonstrates how the past two years have dragged on for Erica.

Explanation = Erica has spent two years working through an extremely routinely life. This is emphasised by the repetition in this phrase.

Question 14

Answer = d) That investors stand to benefit from firms disclosing their diversity statistics.

Explanation = The investors are placing pressure on businesses to disclose diversity statistics. Since the goal of an investor is to make more money, we can infer that there is some kind of financial gain for investors if firms disclose their diversity statistics.

Question 15

Answer = b) There is a correlation between drinking spring water and increased performance in the workplace.

Explanation = Scientists have only found a link between drinking spring water and increased performance. The passage does not state that a causal relationship between the two has been established.

Question 16

Answer = a) That it's a police report of some kind.

Explanation = The formal tone of the passage, combined with the content of the text, strongly suggests that this is some kind of police report.

Question 17

Answer = d) If the Royal Family were to abdicate, the UK would still generate a lot of money through tourism.

Explanation = The passage states that tourism in the UK generates approximately $5 billion per year, whilst the Royal Family generates approximately $800 million of that number. This suggests that, if the Royal Family didn't exist, there would still be $4.2 billion in tourism still being generated.

Question 18

Answer = b) That the company is making a lot of money.

Explanation = This is the main idea of the passage since all of the other ideas in the passage either rely on it or feed into it somehow.

Question 19

Answer = d) This actor is having an impact on what people believe about the refugee crisis.

Explanation = The passage states that a number of activist groups have rallied and are taking action in response to the actor's words. Therefore, this actor is having an impact on what people believe about the refugee crisis.

Question 20

Answer = c) MP3 is on the decline, possible due to the rise of streaming services.

Explanation = Every point in the paragraph feeds into the common idea that MP3 was once popular, but is now on the decline, with the possible reason being that streaming services are now popular.

OAR Mock Test 1 Answers - Mathematical Comprehension Test

Q1. B = 80

EXPLANATION = 120 (total number of people) ÷ 3 = 40. This is equal to $1/_3$. Therefore: 40 x 2 = 80 (this gives you $2/_3$ - which is the number of people who didn't finish the race in under half an hour).

Q2. D = 420

EXPLANATION = 700 ÷ 5 x 3 = 420.

Q3. D = 4

EXPLANATION = there are 1,000 millilitres in 1 litre.That means 4,000 millilitres, would be equivalent to 4 litres.

Q4. C = 100°

EXPLANATION = the angle makes a straight line. A straight line contains angles which add up to 180°.

- So, 180 – 50 – 30 = 100°.

Q5. A = 1,560

EXPLANATION = 120 x 13 = 1,560.

Q6. B = $27

EXPLANATION = $45 ÷ 100 x 60 = $27.

Q7. A = 0

EXPLANATION = this shape is a parallelogram, and these shapes do not contain a line of symmetry. No matter where you draw the reflection line, the shape cannot be reflected symmetrically.

Q8. C = 1,080 g

EXPLANATION = 120 x 9 = 1,080 g. Pay attention to the measurements; the question is in grams (g), so therefore your answer should also be in grams, unless stated otherwise.

Q9. B = 324 cm²

EXPLANATION = the key thing to remember is that the shape is a square (the sides will be the same length). If the perimeter of the shape is 72 cm, that means 72 needs to be divided by 4 (4 sides). So, 72 ÷ 4 = 18. Each length of the square is 18 cm. To work out the area = 18 x 18 = 324 cm².

Q10. D = ½

EXPLANATION = $^{24}/_{48}$, both numbers can be divided by 24. It goes into 24 once, and goes into 48 twice. Therefore it gives the fraction of ½.

Q11. B = 19, 21

EXPLANATION = this is a series of repetition. The regular series adds 2 to every number.

Q12. B = 13, 21

EXPLANATION = this is a Fibonacci number sequence. The sequence follows the pattern of adding the two previous numbers together in order to get the next number. For example, the 8 is found by adding the 5 and the 3 together, and so forth.

Q13. D = 24:17

EXPLANATION = both amounts are in pounds. We have to convert both amounts into pence. £12.00 = 1200p. £8.50 = 850p. Now the ratio is 1200:850. Both sides are divisible by 50. Dividing both sides by 50 gives 24:17. So the ratio is 24:17.

Q14. B = 2:1

EXPLANATION = the answer is 2:1. You can divide both sides of 16:8 by 8.

Q15. A = 14

EXPLANATION = 6 x 7 = 42 ÷ 3 = 14.

Q16. C = 150

EXPLANATION = 120 ÷ 4 = 30 x 5 = 150.

Q17. D = 72

EXPLANATION = 88 ÷ 11 = 8 x 9 = 72.

Q18. C = 7 hours

EXPLANATION = total time spent marking one exam = 6 minutes (Literature) + 7 minutes (Language) + 2 minutes (checking) = 15 minutes. So, 28 exams will take = 15 (minutes) x 28 (exams) = 420 minutes. Converted into hours and minutes = 7 hours.

Q19. D = 90%

EXPLANATION = 0.9 x 100 = 90%.

Q20. B = 6x

EXPLANATION = x + 8x = 9x. So, 9x – 3x = 6x.

Q21. A = 3.7

EXPLANATION = this question asks you to use the method of PEMDAS:

- 2.5 x 8 = 20.

- 23.7 – 20 = 3.7

Q22. C = $^3/_{20}$

EXPLANATION = 20 – 12 – 5 = 3. So your chances of picking a white button is 3 out of a possible 20.

Q23. C = 18

EXPLANATION = 138 ÷ 8 = 17.25. You need one teacher for every 8 students, therefore you would need 18 members of staff in order to cater for 138 students.

Q24. The correct answer would have to look like this:

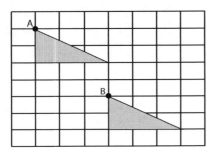

Q25. The correct answer would have to look like this:

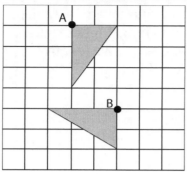

Q26. A = 09:25

EXPLANATION = 08:45 add 15 minutes (form time) = 9 o'clock. 9 o'clock add 25 minutes (assembly time) = 09:25.

Q27. B = $6,000

EXPLANATION = 27 rows of 28 seats = 756 – 5 (that are empty) = 751. 751 (number of seats) x £8 = $6,008. To the nearest hundred = $6,000.

Q28. D = 2,500g

EXPLANATION = there are 1,000g in 1 kilogram. Therefore, 2,500g is equivalent to 2.5 kg (2.5 x 1,000 = 2,500g).

Q29. A = $^9/_{10}$

EXPLANATION = we use decimal points to distinguish whole parts from separate parts (tenths, hundredths, thousandths, etc.). A tenth is $^1/_{10}$ of a unit, therefore the 9 represents 9 tenths of part of a unit.

Q30. C = 30%

EXPLANATION = the set of data is for 10 people. 3 people passed first time so therefore: 10 ÷ 100 x 3 = 0.3 or 0.3 x 100 = 30% or simply 3 out of 10 ($^3/_{10}$).

OAR Mock Test 1 Answers - Mechanical Comprehension Test

Q1. B

When answering questions where there is a single pulley system, if the pulley is fixed, as in A, then the force required to lift the weight is the same as the weight, i.e. 5 kg. However, where the pulley system is not fixed and it moves with the weight, as is the case with pulley system B, then the weight required to lift it is half the weight. This means that the weight required to lift B is 2.5 kg. The answer to the question is therefore B as pulley system A requires the most weight to lift it.

Q2. B

Point X is twice the distance from the balance point; therefore, half the weight is required. The answer is B, 10 kg.

Q3. B

If cog C turns 10 anti-clockwise at a speed of 10 rpm, then it is relatively straightforward to determine that cog B will rotate the same speed but in a clockwise direction.

Q4. A

The only tool that you can use from the selection to claw nails from wood is claw hammer A.

Q5. D

No bulbs would illuminate because the circuit, in its current state, is not working. This is due to the switch being open.

Q6. D

Three bulbs would illuminate.

Q7. A

Cog A will turn clockwise.

Q8. C

Because wheel A is three times greater in diameter than wheel B, each revolution of A will lead to 3 times the revolution of B. Therefore, if wheel A rotates at 55 rpm, B will rotate at 55 rpm × 3 = 165 rpm.

Q9. B

This type of pulley system has a mechanical advantage of 2. Therefore, to lift the 75 kg weight will require 75 kgs ÷ 2 = 37.5 kgs.

Q10. D

There are 8 threads per inch. To move the nut 3 inches will require 8 × 3 = 24 turns.

Q11. A

Each full turn of cog B will result in 18 teeth ÷ 12 teeth = 1.5 rotations. Two turns of cog B will result in cog A completing 3 rotations.

Q12. D

The relative speed of the two cars is 45 m/s + 30 m/s = 75 m/s

Q13. D

In this particular case, frictional force is the force that must be overcome in order to slide the object from one side to another.

Q14. A

An astronaut weighs less on the Moon than Earth because the force of gravity is less on the Moon than on Earth.

Q15. C

By drawing a vertical line straight down from the centre of gravity, only the line for HGV C shows stability. Therefore, this HGV is least likely to fall over.

Q16. D

A seesaw is the only option which utilises a form of leverage to function.

Q17. C

The distance of the weight on the right hand side from the balance point is one third less than the distance on the right hand side; therefore, an additional third weight is required to balance the beam.

Q18. C

In order to balance the beam the weight needs to be placed half the distance of the right hand side (15 feet). This is because the weight on the left is twice as heavy as the weight on the right hand side.

Q19. C

You would need to lift the rope 15 feet in order to lift the weight 5 feet.

Q20. A

Friction is an example of a contact force.

Q21. D

A block and tackle is used to hoist an object upwards by means of rope and pulleys

Q22. A (Man X)

You will see that the object is closer to man Y than man X. Therefore, man X is carrying less weight.

Q23. C

Wheel F and D are the only other wheels which will rotate clockwise.

Q24. C

The working height is 12 metres. The foot of the ladder must be placed 4 metres away from the building. (12 ÷ 3 = 4)

Q25. A

The effort force where the weight is to be applied (where the arrow is pointing) is equal to the resistance weight of the object on the left side of the scales. To work out the mechanical advantage, you can use the following formula: divide the length of the effort by the length of the resistance. So, 32 ÷ 8 = 4. Thus, the mechanical advantage is 4.

Q26. B

The hot air inside a hot air balloon is less dense than the external air.

Q27. A

Balsa wood is the only material here that will float on water.

Q28. C

Water is flowing in at a rate of 18 litres per minute; however, because water is also leaving the tank at a rate of 14 litres per minute, this means that only 4 litres per minute is effectively filling the tank. If the tank has a capacity of 20 litres, then it will take 5 minutes for it to overflow.

Q29. D

In order to calculate the weight required in this type of situation you can make use of the following formula:

- $f = (w \times d1) \div d2$

- f = force required w = weight

- d1 = distance 1 d2 = distance 2

- $f = (50 \times 1) \div 2$

- $(50 \div 2 = 25 \text{ kg})$

Q30. C

It will move left and right as the wheel rotates.

THE OAR TEST - MOCK TEST 2

Note: This chapter contains passages which contain strong opinions on a range of topics. These opinions do not reflect the beliefs of How2Become Ltd or its employees. These opinions are used to create interesting discussion and drive debate.

OAR Mock Test 2 - Reading Comprehension Test

Question 1

All year he's been tormenting me. In fact, I can't actually remember a time where I haven't woken up feeling physically sick at the thought of the abuse that I would be subjected to that day. Even this weekend, the thoughts have spiralled endlessly through my mind. All the things he had said to me that week, to everyone else around me – the humiliation.

Which of the following descriptions best explains the use of the phrase "spiralled endlessly"?

a) This is a metaphor for the constant suffering the narrator has been put through by the bully.

b) This is a simile to describe the way the narrator is feeling.

c) It's designed to make the reader sympathize with the narrator.

d) This is hyperbole, an exaggeration used to highlight how thoughts had occupied the narrator's mind.

Answer

Question 2

Scientific realism is the worldview that scientific disciplines, theories, and successful hypotheses are all working towards some kind of truth. In other words, science is on the right track to objective truth, and regularly makes accurate statements about the world we live in.

Which of the following is an inference which can be drawn from the above passage?

a) Scientific realism is false.

b) Scientific realism also applies to psychology and sociology.

c) According to scientific realism, science is the only way to make accurate statements about the world.

d) Scientific realists believe that we can trust science.

Answer

Question 3

One of the most topical aspects of modern current affairs is that of fake news, a kind of journalism which focuses on the deliberate dissemination of misinformation and hoaxes – usually to serve an agenda. While fake news, even in its strictest definition as deliberate hoax-spreading rather than clumsy rumour-milling, has existed for hundreds of years, it has only started to become part of mainstream political and social discourse during the past two or three years. While this resurgence of chatter regarding fake news might seem like "villain of the week" nonsense to an outsider, our modern social and technological landscape makes fake news a bigger threat than ever.

What is the main idea of the above passage?

a) Fake news is a completely new phenomenon.

b) Hoaxes and rumours have always existed, but modern technology makes fake news a threat.

c) Fake news is a threat.

d) Fake news does not exist.

Answer

Question 4

My city. The beautiful backstreets bustle, and the gorgeous alleyway aroma drifts and flows and fills my nostrils, as I scamper, satisfied, along the cold stone pavements. I feel a rush of warmth inside of me as I catch glimpse of my friends. I see their nude tails whip violently, excitedly, around the corner and I scurry to catch them. To be reunited once again with Todd, Marsha, George and oh...there's my brother, Harry. Why did he have to be here? Regardless, we have the gang all together again, like it should be.

What is the purpose of the above passage being written in the first person?

a) It allows for there to be some mystery regarding the fact that the narrator is not a human being.

b) It allows us to get inside the narrator's head.

c) It tells a more compelling story.

d) It allows for greater description of what the main character is seeing.

Answer

Question 5

The biggest ethical problem which results from the rise of internet personalities is how to handle sponsorship. While traditional celebrities are easy to spot when endorsing a product, it can be harder to distinguish new personalities from the products that they contractually endorse and those that they simply enjoy. When you see a movie star appear in an advert to show off their favourite coffee machine, or a musician endorsing a brand of clothing, you can easily tell that this is the result of a sponsorship deal. While they might genuinely love the product they're endorsing, the audience knows that they are contractually obliged to portray the product in its best light.

Which of the following is an inference which can be made from the above passage?

a) Movie stars get paid more than internet personalities.

b) Sponsorship is always unethical.

c) Unethical sponsorship is more likely to happen amongst internet personalities than movie stars.

d) All movie stars take sponsorship deals.

Answer

Question 6

If the goal of a fictional world is to be entertaining, then the author should use every method at their disposal to do so. In some cases, this might involve breaking internal consistency in order to tell a more meaningful story. For example, a lack of consistency between scenes might demonstrate a communication breakdown between two or more characters, or even be used as a metaphor for one's own internal inconsistency. So, a lack of consistency within a fictional world can create deeper meaning, which might give certain audiences greater enjoyment.

What is the main idea of the above passage?

a) All fiction should aim to be entertaining.

b) All fiction should contain a deeper meaning.

c) It's acceptable to break consistency or logic as long as the piece of fiction is entertaining.

d) Metaphors are an important part of storytelling.

Answer

Question 7

It's undeniable that war is a horrific thing. The pile of bodies, both of civilians and combatants, makes war one of the most reprehensible acts two or more groups of people can commit. Most would argue that our world would be much better without conflict. That said, we can't completely discredit war as pure evil, when it has in fact presented us with many benefits. For example, there are numerous technological and medical advancements which would never have been made were it not for warfare. Penicillin likely wouldn't have been mass-produced were it not for the Second World War, which would mean that the modern world would lack vital antibiotics. Likewise, the x-ray machine was developed because of its usefulness in diagnosing wounds during the First World War.

Which of the following is an inference which can be drawn from the above passage?

a) The First World War is the only war to give us technological advancements.

b) The narrator does not necessarily condone war but appreciates that war results in some positive outcomes.

c) The next war will give us more technological advancements.

d) War is inevitable.

Answer

Question 8

There seems to be an obsession with rejecting one's feelings and opting for a purely logical approach when approaching ethical or practical issues. Perhaps it is a result of renaissance thinking: that each and every one of us is a rational being capable of 'thinking through' all of our problems. Remaining composed is valued above listening to one's own emotions, but where have our ethical theories got us? Whether it's utilitarianism, deontology, or divine command theory, all of our rational means of making ethical decisions are inherently flawed. Emotion, however, remains pure and infallible.

What is the main idea of the above passage?

a) People fret too much about constructing logical ethical systems.

b) Ethical theories are useless in everyday life.

c) Rational thinking is flawed.

d) Emotion is superior to rationality.

Answer

Question 9

History has proven that human beings are poorly suited to large-scale governmental structures and regimes. Whether it's capitalism, socialism, fascism, or feudalism, nation-states with a centralised body are incapable of solving more problems than they cause. Human beings are only capable of caring for a certain amount of people. Once you have a prime minister, president, or dictator taking the reins, they're incapable of empathising with the vast swathes of people that they govern. This leads to all kinds of atrocities. For this reason, nation states should be devolved into a multitude of smaller governing bodies that can focus on serving a more manageable number of people. This form of anarchism is perfect for improving individual happiness.

Which of the following is an inference which can be drawn from the above passage?

a) Fascism is a form of anarchism.

b) Small nation states will not have any leadership.

c) Small anarchist states will fall prey to the same issues that plague larger societies.

d) The writer believes that large nation-states will always face the same issues.

Answer

Question 10

A significant proportion of vegans in the Western world have adopted the lifestyle for ethical reasons. Usually, ethical veganism refers to veganism for animal rights purposes. This definition is used to distinguish it from environmental veganism, and dietary veganism. There are also those who are vegan for purely cultural reasons, with ethical and environmental concerns possessing no influence on their lifestyle choice. However, is ethical veganism really so ethical? While refusing to consume products which are associated with animal cruelty is certainly an ethical decision, it carries implications which aren't so moral. For these reasons, ethical veganism isn't as morally valuable as a vegan would have you believe.

What is the main idea of the above passage?

a) Many vegans choose the lifestyle for ethical reasons. However, the lifestyle might not be as ethical as they believe.

b) All vegans choose the lifestyle for ethical reasons.

c) Ethical veganism is as immoral as eating meat.

d) Veganism has a positive impact on the environment.

Answer

Question 11

A term that you've undoubtedly heard is "by any means necessary". Whether it was in your favourite action movie or from the words of a military dictator, the phrase is so often used that it sometimes doesn't even fully register in our brains. Perhaps we should take a moment to consider what the phrase "by any means necessary" truly stands for.

What is the overall tone of the above passage?

a)   Excited.

b)   Ponderous.

c)   Stern.

d)   Light-hearted.

Answer

Question 12

Ethics is usually focused on people that we have some kind of emotional connection with. Whether it's a comatose relative's wishes to be euthanised, or the morality of abortion, ethical debate is usually focused on matters which are emotionally charged by friendship or love. However, relatives and friends are but a drop in the ocean when compared to the entire world's population. Therefore, we need to consider whether or not we have a moral obligation to people that we've never met, and likely will never meet.

What is the main idea of the above passage?

a) We need to be more considerate towards people we've never met.

b) Ethics is derived from emotion.

c) A central part of ethics involves our relation to others.

d) The world's population is huge.

Answer

Question 13

Triage is a process used by hospital personnel which helps prioritise care and treatment to the variety of patients which arrive in emergency departments. Essentially, it is the practice of assessing patients' condition to figure out who needs medical attention the most.

Triage was first recorded as being used in the Napoleonic Wars, but was reintroduced during the First World War. Triage during the First World War divided patients into the following three categories:

1. Patients who are likely to survive, whether or not they receive care.

2. Patients who are unlikely to survive, whether or not they receive care.

3. Patients whose survival is dependent on the care they imminently receive.

What is the overall tone of the above passage?

a) Inquisitive.

b) Informative.

c) Conversational.

d) Exaggerated.

Answer

Question 14

Many people believe that violence, conflict, and evil are intertwined. Violence is a central part of ethics, with violent behaviour generally being considered immoral. While this is mostly true, it's also a slight simplification of how the world really works. Ideally, all conflict in the world would be avoided altogether, and we should continue to strive for a conflict-free world. Until then, however, there will always be those who use violence as a means of disorder. Sometimes, the only way to prevent this violence is through more violence: albeit more targeted, skilful, and measured. The only way to destroy a terror cell might be to kill its leader, or at least use violent means of capturing them.

What is the main idea of the above passage?

a) Violence is always justified.

b) The world is complex.

c) Sometimes, you have to do morally questionable things to achieve positive outcomes.

d) It's a common belief that violence is wrong.

Answer

Question 15

It has become apparent that over the years, languages have become a dying concept, and society has let this happen. The decline of different languages is clearly linked with political and economic factors that continue to undermine the power of language, and the influence it creates within society. Ultimately, we choose to develop or enhance the language system by applying an effect that will change the overall outcome; whether that outcome is good or not cannot be determined until the effects have taken place, and then it is too late to undo what has already been done.

What is the overall tone of the above passage?

a) Enraged.

b) Sorrowful.

c) Informative.

d) Disaffected.

Answer

Question 16

The proposal to allow younger teenagers to vote in elections is another attempt to turn adolescents into premature adults. Teenagers need time to mature and engage with 'real world' experiences; they have no clear understanding of what the 'real world' entails, nor can they comprehend the importance of making life-changing decisions. It is thought that teenagers should be able to partake in society 100%, because at this age they are able to make life-changing decisions such as leaving home, fighting to serve their country and getting married. Amidst these decisions comes great responsibility; a responsibility that affects only themselves, and therefore by no means should this stand as a reason to allow them to vote in political matters which ultimately impacts everyone on a national level.

What is the main idea of the above passage?

a) Young people do not have enough experience to be responsible as voters.

b) Young people's brains have not fully developed.

c) Voting comes with great responsibility.

d) Teenagers are not mature.

Answer

```



```

Question 17

Human beings have conquered the world. Over the decades, our combined and cumulative efforts have allowed us to map the entire planet. We know so much about the world we live in, and are truly masters of our environments. It's about time we found a new frontier, and given our domination of the lands, it's time that we take to the stars for new adventures and opportunities. The thing that makes us human is our primal urge for discovery. Therefore, we have no choice but to invest in space exploration and travel further than we ever have before.

What is the main idea of the above passage?

a) Human beings have a natural inclination to explore.

b) We should accelerate space exploration.

c) The urge for discovery drives us.

d) We've already mapped the entire world.

Answer

Question 18

English history has witnessed many changes regarding Kings, Queens, traditions, politics, wealth, status and power. Without this history, we would find it difficult to determine our English culture. A particularly influential time within English history was during the Reign of Henry VIII. A conceited, manipulative, assertive and downright power-driven man, Henry became King of England in 1509, following the death of his father and eldest brother. As the author of the book Assertio Septem, which attacked Martin Luther and conversely supported the Roman Catholic Church, Henry VIII was conferred in recognition of his work by the Pope, with the title of Defender of the Faith. In 1515, Henry VIII introduced Thomas Wolsey as Lord Chancellor. From this, Thomas Wolsey became a significant influence in British history. As one of the most powerful ministers in history, he exercised his services through judicial appointments. Hampton Court Palace, which served as the residence of both Wolsey and Henry at different points in their lives, highlights the status of the ruling class at the time.

Which of the following is an inference which can be drawn from the above passage?

a) Henry VIII was sympathetic to Catholicism.

b) Henry VIII was a devout Protestant.

c) Henry VIII was third in line to the throne after his father.

d) Henry VIII was a much-loved king.

Answer

Question 19

Social networking has unquestionably become a global phenomenon, which I believe is having a huge effect on our social world. Social networking sites such as Facebook and Twitter have experienced exponential growth during the 21st century, and yet some users remain oblivious to how much their social networking profiles can shape, influence and affect their everyday lives.

What is the overall tone of this passage?

a) Condescending.

b) Assertive.

c) Conversational.

d) Informative.

Answer

Question 20

We live in a world that is constantly changing. As human beings, we are constantly making new scientific discoveries, and producing theories, contemplations and ideas on how we began our existence. One of these theories is string theory. In an attempt to explain all of the fundamentals of nature, superstring theory analyses the vibrations of tiny supersymmetric strings. For example, let's compare string theory with a guitar in order to gain a clearer understanding of how string theory actually works. A guitar is tuned by the stretching and tweaking of strings, which are put under tension to form vibrations and create sound. The musical note that is played, depends on how that string is plucked, where you position your hands, and how much tension the strings are under. This is very similar to the way in which string theory works.

Which of the following is an inference which can be drawn from the above passage?

a)   String theory is a relatively new scientific theory.

b)   String theory behaves identically to how a guitar string works.

c)   String theory has been proven.

d)   String theory is controversial.

Answer

OAR Mock Test 2 - Mathematical Comprehension Test

You have 40 minutes to answer the following 30 questions.

Question 1

Work out $\dfrac{2}{5} + \dfrac{7}{8}$

A	B	C	D
$5\frac{7}{8}$	$1\frac{11}{40}$	$2\frac{12}{30}$	$1\frac{10}{40}$

Question 2

Work out $\dfrac{4}{6} \times \dfrac{3}{5}$

A	B	C	D
$\frac{1}{5}$	$\frac{3}{5}$	$\frac{4}{5}$	$\frac{2}{5}$

Question 3

Below is a diagram of a cube. Work out its volume in cubic centimetres.

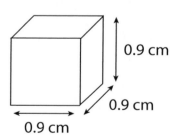

0.9 cm

0.9 cm

0.9 cm

A	B	C	D
729cm³	0.729cm³	0.7cm³	0.65cm³

Question 4

Three whole numbers add up to a total of 100. The first number is a multiple of 15. The second number is ten times the third number. Both the second and the third number are a multiple of 5. Work out the three numbers.

A	B	C	D
40, 60, and 10	120, 140, 30	45, 50, and 5	15, 45, 5

Question 5

The probability of picking a lottery winning ticket in the national lottery is 1 in 14 million. If 36 million tickets are sold weekly, how many jackpot winners, on average, would you expect in one week?

A	B	C	D
2,000,000	2	20	1

Question 6

A car travelled 100 metres in 9.63 seconds. On a second occasion, it travelled 200 metres in 19.32 seconds. Which distance had the greater average speed?

A	B	C	D
100 metres	200 metres	Both the same	Cannot say

Question 7

A function is represented by the following machine.

Input ——— [x 7] ——— [- 6] ——— Output

A number is put into the machine. The output of the machine is 71. What was the number inputted into the machine?

A	B	C	D
32	7	15	11

Question 8

What is one quarter of 6 hours?

A	B	C	D
1 hour and 30 minutes	95 minutes	180 minutes	1 hour and 20 minutes

Question 9

Simplify $5w - 5x - 4w - 2x$.

A	B	C	D
$1w - 7x$	$25x - 8w$	$10w - 10x$	$8x - 25w$

Question 10

A function is represented by the following machine.

9 is put into the machine. The output of the machine is 126. What is the missing function in the second part of the machine sequence?

A	B	C	D
Divide by 12	Multiply by 6	Multiply by 3	Divide by 6

Question 11

Which of the following is **not** a factor of 48?

A	B	C	D
12	8	14	16

Question 12

What month saw the mode number of pupils to be absent in the one month period, across all five subjects?

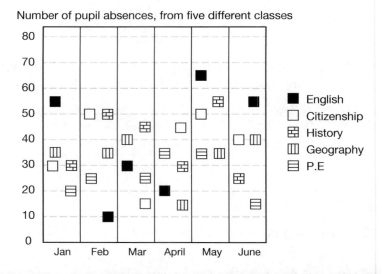

Number of pupil absences, from five different classes

A	B	C	D
February	May	June	March

Question 13

How many different numbers can be made from these four playing cards?

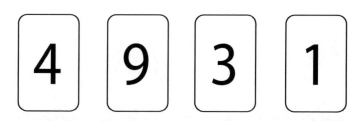

A	B	C	D
24	22	18	7

Question 14

A Science exam is marked out of 50. There are 30 pupils in the class. The marks of the class are as follows:

7	36	41	22	36	22
41	27	29	30	20	17
9	32	47	43	31	29
27	29	32	9	28	35
17	12	8	34	27	29

Using this stem and leaf diagram, add the data in ascending order.

```
   |
0  |
   |
1  |
   |
2  |
   |
3  |
   |
4  |
   |
5  |
```

Question 15

Using the above stem and leaf diagram, what is the median?

A	B	C	D
30	29	25	8

Question 16

Work out the angle C.

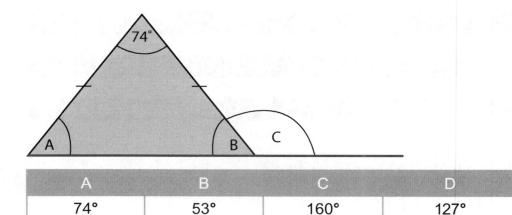

A	B	C	D
74°	53°	160°	127°

Question 17

Calculate 158 x 67.

A	B	C	D
10,586	12,210	15,800	33,250

Question 18

A farmer has 630 eggs. They are to be placed in egg trays. Each tray can hold 36 eggs. How many trays will be needed to hold all of the eggs?

A	B	C	D
15	36	18	17.5

Question 19

Mark is going to make chocolate peanut squares. There are just three ingredients: chocolate, peanut butter, and rice pops. This is mixed in the ratio 4 : 2 : 3 respectively.

How much peanut butter will he need to make 900 g of mixture?

A	B	C	D
450g	200g	400g	300g

Question 20

Two of the numbers move from Box A to Box B. The total of the numbers in Box B is now four times the total of the numbers in Box A. Which two numbers move?

Box A   **Box B**

A	B	C	D
4 and 8	9 and 4	6 and 1	2 and 5

Question 21

Work out 256% of 6,800.

A	B	C	D
16,800	12,400	15,000	17,408

Question 22

Subtract $^3/_8$ of 104 from $^5/_7$ of 98.

A	B	C	D
27	22	31	41

Question 23

Below is a pie chart illustrating the number of pupils studying a course in the following subject areas.

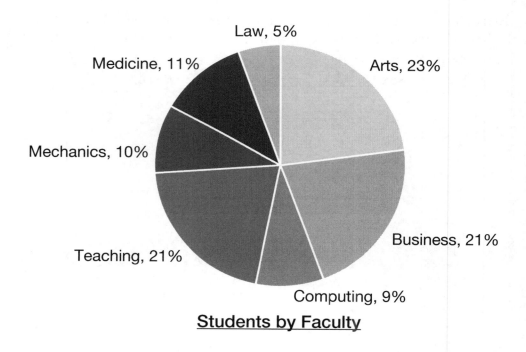

Students by Faculty

If the data is based on 3,620 students, how many of those students are studying either mechanics or law?

A	B	C	D
543	181	200	460

Question 24

Below is a bar chart displaying some of the heights of the highest mountains.

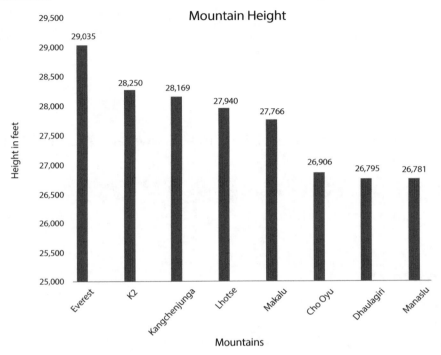

Work out the average height, to the nearest hundred, based on the information provided.

A	B	C	D
27,770	28,000	27,800	27,700

Question 25

Which two numbers come next?

2, 4, 8, 16, 32, 64, ...

A	B	C	D
126 and 215	128 and 256	128 and 265	182 and 265

Question 26

Lisa cycles at an average speed of 8 km/h. How far (in kilometers) does she travel if she cycles for 4 hours?

A	B	C	D
32km	26km	35km	45km

Question 27

James runs from 4.50pm until 5.20pm at an average speed of 7 km/h. How far did he go?

A	B	C	D
7km	15km	5km	3.5km

Question 28

What is the highest common factor of 12 and 20?

A	B	C	D
4	8	12	2

Question 29

Here is a spinner. Circle the chance of the spinner landing on an odd number.

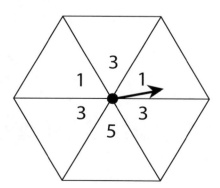

A	B	C	D
$\frac{6}{6}$ or 1	$\frac{4}{6}$	$\frac{1}{2}$	$\frac{1}{3}$

Question 30

What is the angle of D?

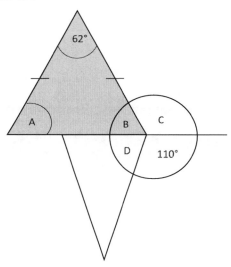

A	B	C	D
90°	62°	70°	60°

OAR Mock Test 2 - Mechanical Comprehension Test

You have 15 minutes to answer the following 30 questions.

Question 1

If wheel A turns in an anti-clockwise direction, which way will wheel B turn?

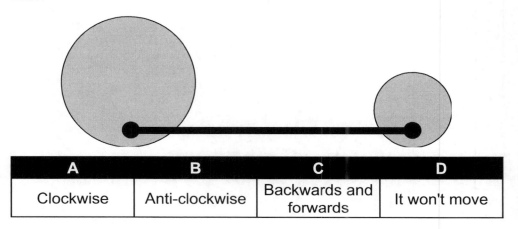

A	B	C	D
Clockwise	Anti-clockwise	Backwards and forwards	It won't move

Question 2

Which post is carrying the least heavy load?

A. Post A

B. Post B

Question 3

Which pendulum will swing at the fastest speed rate?

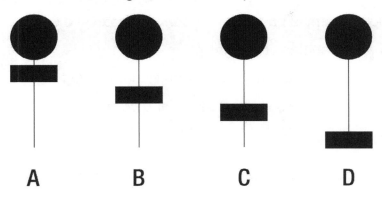

A	B	C	D
Pendulum A	Pendulum B	Pendulum C	Pendulum D

Question 4

If Cog B turns clockwise, which of the other cogs will also turn clockwise?

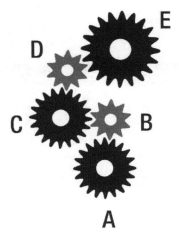

A	B	C	D
Cogs D and C	Cogs A, C and E	Cog D	Cogs D and E

Question 5

The use of an earth-fault loop test is to make sure that...

A. Enough current is passable to open the protective device.

B. No charge can pass through.

C. The voltage through the circuit remains low.

D. The earth wire is connected safely and correctly.

Question 6

Which shelf will break first when a heavy load is placed on the whole shelf?

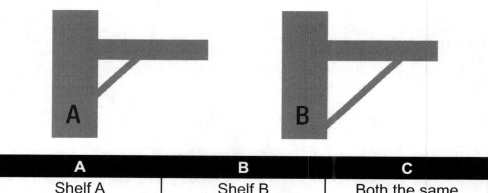

A	B	C
Shelf A	Shelf B	Both the same

Question 7

At which point will the pendulum be travelling at the fastest speed?

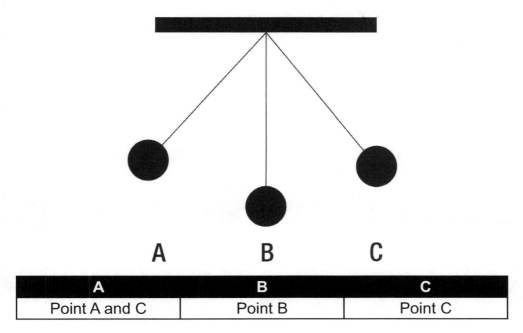

A	B	C
Point A and C	Point B	Point C

Question 8

At which point will the beam balance?

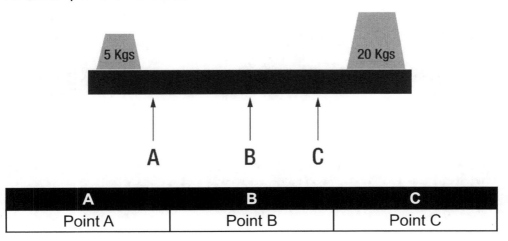

A	B	C
Point A	Point B	Point C

Question 9

If water is poured into the narrow tube, up to point 'X', what height would it reach in the wide tube?

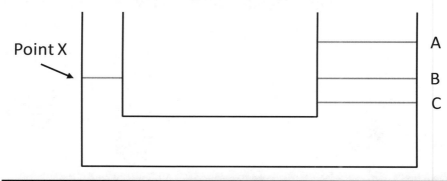

A	B	C
Point A	Point B	Point C

Question 10

Ball X and Ball Y are both made from the same material. At which point would Ball Y have to be placed to balance Ball X?

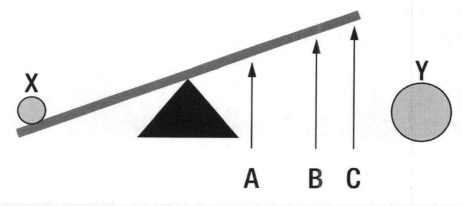

A	B	C
Point A	Point B	Point C

Question 11

If Cog F rotates clockwise, which way will Cog A turn?

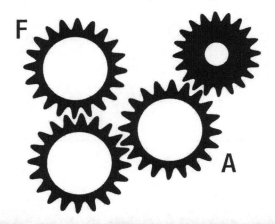

A	B	C
Cannot say	Clockwise	Anti-clockwise

Question 12

What is the mechanical advantage?

A	B	C	D
1	2	3	4

Question 13

If water is poured in at Point D, which tube will overflow first?

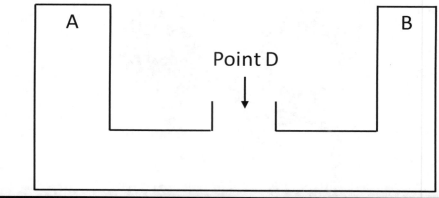

A	B	C
Tube A	Both the same	Tube B

Question 14

What is the mechanical advantage?

A	B	C	D
1	2	3	4

Question 15

If rope A is pulled in the direction of the arrow, which way will wheel C turn?

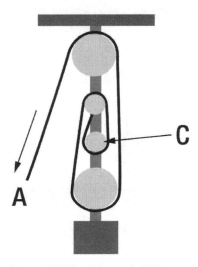

A	B	C
Clockwise	Anti-clockwise	It will not turn

Question 16

Which load is the heaviest?

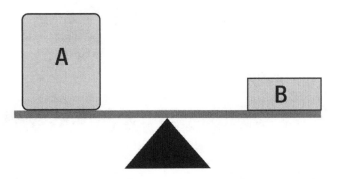

A	B	C
Both the same	Load B	Load A

Question 17

Which pulley system is a moveable pulley system?

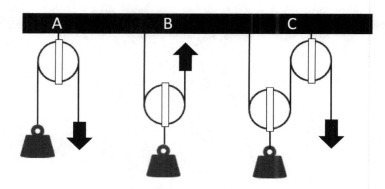

A	B	C
Pulley A	Pulley B	Pulley C

Question 18

If cog A turns anticlockwise at a speed of 20 rpm (revolutions per minute), how will cog B turn?

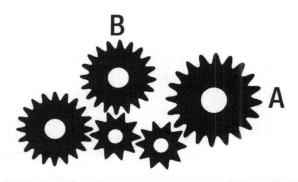

A	B	C	D
Clockwise, 20 rpm	Anti-clockwise, 20 rpm	Clockwise, 10 rpm	Anti-clockwise, 10 rpm

Question 19

Which pulley system will be the easiest to lift the bucket of water?

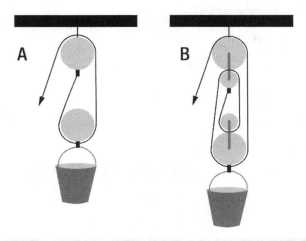

A	B	C
Both the same	Pulley A	Pulley B

Question 20

Ball A and B are an identical size and weight. If they are both released at the same time, what will happen?

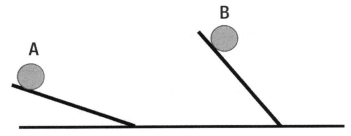

A. Ball A will reach the ground first.

B. Ball B will reach the ground first.

C. They will both reach the ground at the same time.

Question 21

How much weight in kg should be placed at the location of question mark to balance the weights?

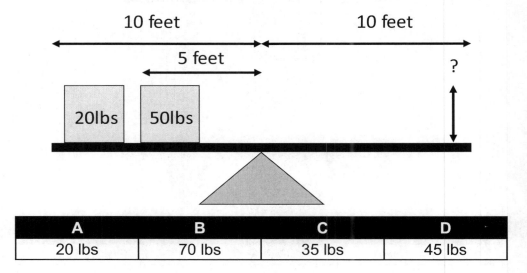

A	B	C	D
20 lbs	70 lbs	35 lbs	45 lbs

Question 22

What would happen to a balloon full of air, if you were to place it 15 feet below a water surface?

A. The volume of the balloon would increase.

B. The volume of the balloon would stay the same.

C. The balloon would explode.

D. The volume of the balloon would decrease.

Question 23

In the diagram, the spring can be stretched 1 inch by a force of 200 pounds. How much force needs to be applied to the object in order to move the object 4.5 inches to the left?

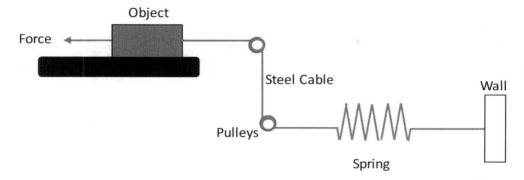

A	B	C	D
900 pounds	450 pounds	800 pounds	90 pounds

Question 24

Which type of beam can take the greatest load?

A	B	C
Beam A	Beam B	Both the same

Question 25

If gear A in the diagram begins spinning clockwise, what will happen to the spring that is attached to the wall?

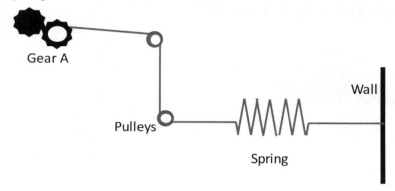

A	B	C	D
The spring will be compressed	The spring will stretch	The spring will touch the gears	Nothing

Question 26

Which crane is working under the least tension?

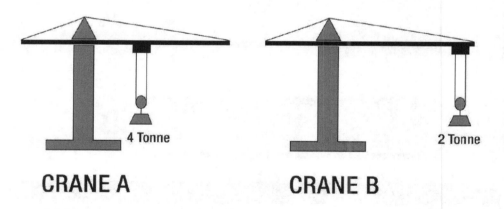

A	B	C
Crane A	Crane B	Both the same

Question 27

Which of the following should be tightened by hand?

A. Bolt
B. Machine screw
C. Wing nut
D. Wood screw

Question 28

A ball is attached to a piece of string which in turn is secured to a ceiling. The ball and string are then held close to your nose but do not touch it. The ball and string are then released and allowed to swing away from you. When they swing back towards you, will they touch your face if you remain still?

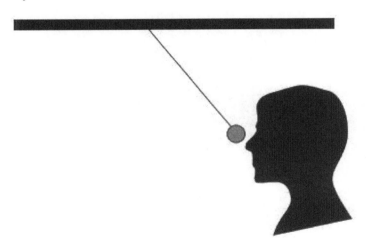

A. Yes
B. No

Question 29

Which spanner will it be harder to tighten the bolt with?

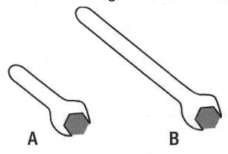

A	B	C
Spanner A	Spanner B	Both the same

Question 30

If the large piston has 4 times the surface area of the small piston, how far must the small piston be pushed down in order to raise the large piston 1cm?

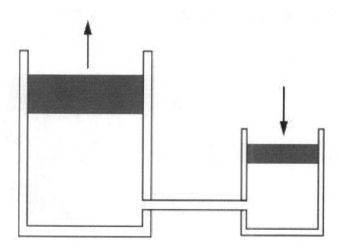

A	B	C	D
0.5cm	1cm	2cm	4cm

OAR MOCK TEST 2 - ANSWERS

OAR Mock Test 2 Answers - Reading Comprehension Test

Question 1

Answer = d) This is hyperbole, an exaggeration used to highlight how thoughts had occupied the narrator's mind.

Explanation = The thoughts were not spiralling 'endlessly' in the narrator's mind. Therefore, it must be assumed that this is hyperbole.

Question 2

Answer = d) Scientific realists believe that we can trust science.

Explanation = Scientific realism is the belief that science makes accurate statements about the world. Therefore, it's reasonable to infer that scientific realists believe that we can trust science.

Question 3

Answer = b) Hoaxes and rumours have always existed, but modern technology makes fake news a threat.

Explanation = All of the other ideas in this passage relate to the above statement in some way.

Question 4

Answer = d) It allows for greater description of what the main character is seeing.

Explanation = The purpose of first person writing is to give the reader a better insight into the experiences, thoughts and feelings of the character - to help them to see the world from that character's perpspective.

Question 5

Answer = c) Unethical sponsorship is more likely to happen amongst internet personalities than movie stars.

Explanation = The passage identifies an ethical issue regarding the rise of internet personalities as sponsorship. The passage than goes on to compare internet personalities to movie stars. From this, we can infer that unethical sponsorship is more likely to occur amongst internet personalities than movie stars.

Question 6

Answer = c) It's acceptable to break consistency or logic as long as the piece of fiction is entertaining.

Explanation = All of the statements in the passage all feed in to this central concept.

Question 7

Answer = b) The narrator does not necessarily condone war but appreciates that war results in some positive outcomes.

Explanation = The narrator or author acknowledges that "war is a horrific thing". However, they also make note that medical and technological progress comes out of war.

Question 8

Answer = d) Emotion is superior to rationality.

Explanation = The author emphasises emotion's superiority over rationality throughout the passage. As far we can tell, it appears to be the central thread of the argument.

Question 9

Answer = d) The writer believes that large nation-states will always face the same issues.

Explanation = The writer argues that anarchism is better than large nations because smaller bodies face less of the issues that large nations do. The writer argues that we should change to anarchism as a model for society. Therefore, the author is implying that large nation-states can never overcome their problems.

Question 10

Answer = a) Many vegas choose the lifestyle for ethical reasons. However, the lifestyle might not be as ethical as they believe.

Explanation = All of the ideas in this passage rely on, or point to, this statement.

Question 11

Answer = b) Ponderous.

Explanation = Terms such as "perhaps" and "moment to consider" give the impression that the author wants to invoke deep though on the issue, making it seem ponderous.

Question 12

Answer = c) A central part of ethics involves our relation to others.

Explanation = This is a central idea which persists throughout the entire passage.

Question 13

Answer = b) Informative.

Explanation = The passage uses formal language and a numbered list to present information. Therefore, it can be considered to have an informative tone.

Question 14

Answer = c) Sometimes, you have to do morally questionable things to achieve positive outcomes.

Explanation = The passage is focused on the utilitarian principle of creating happiness for the greatest number. In some cases, this involves killing people to protect innocents. Therefore, the main idea of this passage is that sometimes you have to do morally questionable things to achieve positive outcomes.

Question 15

Answer = b) Sorrowful.

Explanation = This entire passage laments the death of different languages, and also states that nothing can be done about it. Therefore, it can be said that the tone is sorrowful.

Question 16

Answer = a) Young people do not have enough experience to be responsible as voters.

Explanation = The entirety of this passage is predicated on the above idea. Therefore, it can be considered the main idea of the passage.

Question 17

Answer = b) We should accelerate space exploration.

Explanation = The passage reiterates that it's natural for humans to explore, and therefore we should explore space. Therefore, the main idea of this passage is that we should accelerate and invest in space exploration.

Question 18

Answer = c) Henry VIII was third in line to the throne after his father.

Explanation = According to the passage, Henry became king after both his father and brother died. Therefore, he was third in line to the throne after his father.

Question 19

Answer = b) Assertive.

Explanation = The writer takes the voice of the first person, using the term "I" to own their argument. Therefore, it's reasonable to say that the tone of the passage is assertive.

Question 20

Answer = a) String theory is a relatively new scientific theory.

Explanation = The passage states that "we are constantly making new scientific discoveries, and producing theories" before introducing string theory. This implies that string theory is a relatively new scientific theory.

OAR Mock Test 2 Answers - Mathematical Comprehension Test

Q1. B = $\frac{11}{40}$

EXPLANATION = $\frac{2}{5} \times \frac{7}{8} = \frac{16 + 35}{40} = \frac{51}{40}$ or $1\frac{11}{40}$

Q2. D = 2/5

EXPLANATION = $\frac{4}{6} \times \frac{3}{5} = \frac{4 \times 3}{6 \times 5} = \frac{12}{30}$ or $\frac{6}{15}$ or $\frac{2}{5}$

Q3. B = 0.729 cm³

EXPLANATION = 0.9 x 0.9 x 0.9 = 0.729 cm³

Q4. C = 45, 50 and 5

EXPLANATION = three numbers with two of these criteria: a multiple of 15, two numbers in the ratio 10 : 1, and sum of 100.

- Multiples of 15 = 15, 30, 45, 60, 75, 90. So, the first number will be one of these numbers. Two of the numbers follow the rule of: being in the ratio 10 : 1. This works out to be 50 and 5, and will add up to 100 if you add the 45.

Q5. B = 2

EXPLANATION = 36 (million) ÷ 14 (million) = 2.57. So you could expect

2 lottery winners, on average, in a week.

Q6. A = 100 metres

EXPLANATION = $100 \div 9.63 = 10.384$. $200 \div 19.32 = 10.351$. Therefore 100 metres has the greatest average speed.

Q7. D = 11

EXPLANATION = $71 + 6 \div 7 = 11$. (Remember, to work out the original number, you must work backwards. In order for you to work backwards, you must do the opposite to what the machine is telling you to do).

Q8. A = 1 hour and 30 minutes

EXPLANATION = 6 (hours) x 60 (minutes) = 360 minutes. So, 360 (minutes) $\div$ 4 ($\frac{1}{4}$) = 90 minutes.

Q9. A = 1w − 7x

EXPLANATION = you need to break up the sequence: (5w) (-5x) (-4w) (-2x).

So, 5w − 4w = 1w and -5x − 2x = -7x. So this simplifies to: 1w − 7x.

Q10. B = Multiply by 6

EXPLANATION = $9 + 12 = 21$. $126 \div 21 = 6$. Therefore if you put (x6) into the equation (because you divided 126 by 6, you would put the opposite into the equation). Therefore, 9 + 12 x 6 = 126.

Q11. C = 14

EXPLANATION = the definition of factors is 'all the numbers that can be divided into that number', i.e. what numbers can be multiplied together to reach that number?

Q12. B = May

EXPLANATION = you need to add up all of the subjects for each month. January = 170, February = 170, March = 155, April = 145, May = 240, June = 175. Therefore the mode (the most) in one given month is in May.

Q13. A = 24

EXPLANATION = starting with the number 4, you can get 6 numbers (4931, 4913, 4319, 4391, 4139, 4193). This can be done for all 4 numbers (if you start with a different number; you will be able to make 6 different numbers). Therefore 6 groups of 4 = 24.

Q14. Your answer should look exactly like this:

0	7 8 9 9
1	2 7 7
2	0 2 2 7 7 7 8 9 9 9 9
3	0 1 2 2 4 5 6 6
4	1 1 3 7
5	

Q15. B = 29

EXPLANATION = putting the data in order from smallest to biggest, you then need to find the median (middle) number. Do this by eliminating one number from the start, and one number from the end, until you reach the number in the middle. For this sequence, two numbers are left in the middle: 29 and 29. So, add both numbers and divide it by 2 to find the middle number. So, 29 + 29 ÷ 2 = 29.

Q16. D = 127°

EXPLANATION = a triangle contains 180°. So, 180 - 74° = 106°. Both A and B are going to be the same size (you will notice two small lines placed on both sides of the triangle, illustrating they're the same size and length). So, 106 ÷ 2 = 53°. To work out angle C, a straight line has 180°. You've just worked out angle B is 53°, so 180° − 53° = 127°.

Q17. A = 10,586

EXPLANATION = first, multiply by 7 (units): 158 x 7 = 1,106. Then add a zero on the right side of the next row. This is because we want to multiply by 60 (6 tens), which is the same as multiplying by 10 and by 6. Now multiply by 6: 158 x 60 = 9,480. Now add the two rows together: 9,480 + 1106 = 10,586.

Q18. C = 18

EXPLANATION = 630 ÷ 36 = 17.5. So, you would need 18 trays in order to hold all the eggs.

Q19. C = 200g

EXPLANATION = to work out the chocolate: 900 ÷ 100 x 4 = 400g. To work out the peanut butter = 900 ÷ 100 x 2 = 200g. To work out the rice pops = 900 ÷ 100 x 3 = 300g.

Q20. B = 9 and 4

EXPLANATION = if you moved 9 and 4, this leaves Box A with a total of 11. If you add 9 and 4 to 10, 1 7, 8 and 5, you will get 44. Therefore, this is 4 times as many.

Q21. D = 17,408

EXPLANATION = 6,800 ÷ 100 x 256 = 17,408.

Q22. C = 31

EXPLANATION =

104 ÷ 8 x 3 = 39.

98 ÷ 7 x 5 = 70.

So, 70 – 39 = 31.

Q23. A = 543

EXPLANATION = 3,620 ÷ 100 x 5 = 181 (Law students). 3,620 ÷ 100 x 10 = 362 (Mechanical students). So, the number of law and mechanical students is: 362 + 181 = 543.

Q24. D = 27,700

EXPLANATION = add up all of the sums and divide it by how many mountains there are (8). So, 29,035 + 28,250 + 28,169 + 27,940 + 27,766 + 26,906 + 26,795 + 26,781 = 22,1642 ÷ 8 = 27,705.25. To the nearest hundred = 27,700.

Q25. B = 128 and 256

EXPLANATION = the sequence follows the pattern of 'the power of 2'. In other words, the number is multiplied by 2 each time. So, 64 x 2 = 128 and 128 x 2 = 256.

Q26. A = 32 km

EXPLANATION = Speed x time. So, 8 x 4 = 32 km.

Q27. D = 3.5 km

EXPLANATION = the difference between 4.50pm and 5.20pm = 30 minutes. 30 minutes = 0.5 hour. Remember, distance = speed x time. So, distance = 7 x 0.5 = 3.5 km.

Q28. A = 4

EXPLANATION = the factors of 12 are: 1, 2, 3, 4, 6 and 12. The factors of 20 are: 1, 2, 4, 5, 10 and 20. So the highest common factor of 12 and 20 is 4.

Q29. A = $^6/_6$ or 1.

EXPLANATION = the spinner contains only odd numbers. So no matter what number it lands on, you will always spin an odd number.

Q30. C = 70°

EXPLANATION = $180° - 62° = 118°$. So $118° \div 2 = 59°$. So angles A and B are 59°.

To work out angle C = $180° - 59° = 121°$

Then angle D is $360° - 121° - 59° - 110° = 70°$

OAR Mock Test 2 Answers - Mechanical Comprehension Test

Q1. A

Because the two wheels are joined they will rotate the same way. If A rotates anticlockwise, wheel B will also.

Q2. A

Post A is carrying the least heavy load as the majority of force is placed on post B.

Q3. A

Pendulum A will swing at the fastest speed rate. The lower down the weight, the slower the pendulum will swing.

Q4. C

Cog D is the only other cog which will rotate clockwise.

Q5. A

An earth-fault loop test is used to determine the current so that is is able to flow if an earth fault arises, which allows for the protective device to be opened.

Q6. A

Shelf A will break first, simply because the supporting bar is at a shallower angle than B.

Q7. B

Point B will be the fastest speed. At points A and C the pendulum will be reaching, or have reached, its maximum velocity before falling back down.

Q8. C

In order to balance the beam the point of balance will move closer to the heavier weight. In this case the 20 Kg weight.

Q9. B

The water will rise to the same level on the opposite side as point X.

Q10. A

In order to balance the beam Ball Y will need to be placed closer to the fulcrum point.

Q11. B

Cog A will rotate clockwise.

Q12. C

The mechanical advantage of this pulley system is 3. There are three supporting ropes.

Q13. B

Both entrance and exit points of the container are level, therefore, both will overflow at the same time.

Q14. D

The mechanical advantage of this pulley system is 4. There are four supporting ropes.

Q15. B

Wheel C will rotate anti-clockwise if rope A is pulled in the direction shown.

Q16. A

Both loads are of equal weight. Do not fall in to the trap of thinking load A is heavier simply because it looks larger. The key to answering this question is to look at the balancing bar. You will see that in this case it is level, meaning that both loads weigh the same.

Q17. B

Pulley system B is a moveable pulley system.

Q18. A

Cog B will turn clockwise at a speed of 20 rpm.

Q19. C

Pulley B will be the easiest to lift the load. Pulley A has a mechanical advantage of 2 whereas pulley B has a mechanical advantage of 4.

Q20. B

Although the distance each ball has to travel is identical, ball B will hit the ground first because the incline is steeper.

Q21. D

f = (20 x 10) + (50 x 5) ÷ 10

f = (200) + (250) ÷ 10

f = 450 ÷ 10 = 45 lbs

Q22. D

If you were to place a balloon full of air 15 feet under a water surface, the volume of the balloon would decrease. According to Boyle's Law, the pressure on the balloon from the water would press inwards, and therefore it would cause the balloon to shrink in size and subsequently decrease the volume of the balloon.

Q23. A

4.5 x 200 = 900 pounds

Q24. A

Beam A is the strongest because each triangular section covers a greater surface area.

Q25. A

If the gears moved in a clockwise manner, that means the cable connecting everything together is going to move right (towards the wall), and so the spring will be compressed.

Q26. C

They are both under the same tension. Although the weight lifted by crane A is double that of crane B, the distance between the weight and the centre of gravity is equal for both crane A and crane B.

Q27. C

A wing nut should be tightened by hand.

Q28. B

They will not touch your face because there is insufficient speed or force for the ball to travel further than the point of origin.

Q29. A

Spanner A will be harder to tighten the bolt with, simply because the smaller handle creates less leverage.

Q30. D

Because the larger piston is 4 times the surface area, the smaller piston will need to pushed down 4cm in order to move the large piston 1cm.

A FEW FINAL
WORDS...

You have now reached the end of your guide to the US Navy OAR test, and no doubt you feel more prepared to tackle the OAR exam. We hope you have found this guide an invaluable insight into the test, and understand the expectations regarding your assessment.

For any type of test, we believe there are a few things to remember in order to better your chances and increase your overall performance.

REMEMBER – THE THREE Ps!

Preparation. This may seem relatively obvious, but you will be surprised by how many people fail their assessment because they lacked preparation and knowledge regarding their test. You want to do your utmost to guarantee the best possible chance of succeeding. Be sure to conduct as much preparation prior to your assessment to ensure you are fully aware and 100% prepared to complete the test successfully. Not only will practising guarantee to better your chances of successfully passing, but it will also make you feel at ease by providing you with knowledge and know-how to pass your OAR exam.

Perseverance. You are far more likely to succeed at something if you continuously set out to achieve it. Everybody comes across times whereby they are setback or find obstacles in the way of their goals. The important thing to remember when this happens, is to use those setbacks and obstacles as a way of progressing. It is what you do with your past experiences that helps to determine your success in the future. If you fail at something, consider 'why' you have failed. This will allow you to improve and enhance your performance for next time.

Performance. Your performance will determine whether or not you are likely to succeed. Attributes that are often associated with performance are *self-belief, motivation* and *commitment.* Self-belief is important for anything you do in life. It allows you to recognise your own abilities and skills and believe that you can do well. Believing that you can do well is half the battle! Being fully motivated and committed is often difficult for some people, but we can assure you that, nothing is gained without hard work and determination. If you want to succeed, you will need to put in that extra time and hard work!

Good luck with your OAR test. We wish you the best of luck with all your future endeavours!

The How2Become Team

FOR MORE CAREERS GUIDANCE GO TO:

WWW.HOW2BECOME.COM